RELIGIOUS

TELEVISION

PROGRAMS

PLaza 9-6800

ROY DANISH
Director

TELEVISION INFORMATION OFFICE
of the National Association of Broadcasters
745 Fifth Avenue, New York, N. Y. 10022

RELIGIOUS
TELEVISION
PROGRAMS

A Study of Relevance

By

A. William Bluem

COMMUNICATION ARTS BOOKS

Hastings House, Publishers • *New York*

television in religion

PUBLISHED SIMULTANEOUSLY IN CANADA
BY SAUNDERS OF TORONTO, LTD.
DON MILLS, ONTARIO

SBN: 8038–6298–9
LIBRARY OF CONGRESS CATALOGUE CARD NUMBER: 68–31687
PRINTED IN THE UNITED STATES OF AMERICA

CONTENTS

FOREWORD

For the religious broadcaster, there are two kinds of potential viewer: the committed and the disengaged. Here lies the dilemma for the churchman-on-the-air. Shall he reach out for those who already reach toward him? Or shall he risk precious time in the all-too-often failing effort to capture and hold the interest of the uninterested.

Were there few efforts made, this book and the study on which it was based would be a needless exercise. But, in fact, stations and networks originate a stream of sermons and discussions, homilies and exhortations, dramas-in-dance and dramas-in-prose. The value of time and energy given by broadcasters to local and national churches exceeds a million dollars each week. Additional programs arc paid for by sponsoring churches, although more than half the stations responding in this study will not accept sponsored religious programs.

How does one measure the impact of these many attempts to reach man where he is least accessible? Program ratings? They say little except that audiences are small even by modest mass media

standards. Church attendance? There's little encouragement here
(crisis is the great filler of pews). Audience mail? Unfortunately,
few viewers take the time to write when they find a broadcast
commendable.

As you follow Dr. Bluem's examination of religious broadcasting, bear in mind two time-tested axioms of those who communicate through mass media. First, these media reinforce beliefs far
more effectively than they change them, because all of us defend
our pre-conceptions with a tenacity which defies the powers of the
mass media. Second, television, if it is to hold our attention for
more than a passing moment, must speak to us in our own terms
and address itself to our needs as we ourselves see them.

The religious broadcaster succeeds or fails to the extent that
he recognizes and builds on these premises. He has many alterna-
tive creative solutions among which to find those appropriate to
his own objectives. But he must first be a good broadcaster if he
is to be an effective religious broadcaster. How often he succeeds
or fails and how he may succeed more often are the subjects of
this book.

Roy Danish, DIRECTOR
Television Information Office

AUTHOR'S NOTE

The Author wishes to express his thanks to his editorial staff, to the Television Information Office, and to the Editors of two earlier volumes in this series—*Interaction* and *For the Young Viewer*—who established worthy and useful examples for his task.

Syracuse, N. Y.   A. Wm. Bluem
March, 1969

A. WILLIAM BLUEM served as the Editor of *Television Quarterly,* the highly respected journal of the The National Academy of Television Arts and Sciences from its inception in 1961 to 1968. He earned his Ph.D. at the Ohio State University in 1959, and was a visiting scholar in Film and the Psychology of Mass Communications at the University of Southern California and University of California at Los Angeles. He is the only university teacher in the U. S. to be awarded Honorary Life Membership in The National Academy of Television Arts and Sciences. Dr. Bluem is a co-author of *Television in the Public Interest* (1961), author of *Documentary in American Television* (1965) and a co-editor of *Television: The Creative Experience* (1967), all published by Hastings House. At present a Professor in the Newhouse Communications Center at Syracuse University, Dr. Bluem conducts graduate seminars in Public Communication.

RELIGIOUS

TELEVISION

PROGRAMS

. . . To be relevant today, religion must support those human aspirations that cry for fulfillment in terms of the modern technological capacity. It must become relevant to the effort toward a more abundant life for man. It must teach not only the appropriateness of justice, wisdom, fortitude, and courage, but it must also bear witness to a faith, hope and charity rendered relevant to the new world man has made and the new man whose promise it contains.

—Thomas F. O'Dea
"The Crisis of Contemporary
Religious Consciousness"
Daedalus, Winter, 1967.

I

RELIGION AND BROADCASTING

Notes on the Varieties of Relevance

THE INSTITUTIONS of religion and public communication in every modern industrial nation are confronted with severe challenges in performing their traditional functions. The age of electricity has generated startling concepts of how man must perform new social roles if he is to assure the progress of society—at the same time heeding a constant inner demand to define his moral position and articulate his values in relation to the rapidly-changing situations into which the society has thrust him. The churches and the mass media alike are pressed to help mankind meet these demands.

Even the most tentative examination of contemporary spiritual and social issues reveals widespread anxiety over such concerns as the changing structure of our morals and mores, the seeming proliferation of crime, those dangers inherent in population growth for a sheer "massness" of man, the disturbing expressions of conflict between generations, the often angry thrust toward cultural identity by minority groups and the poverty-stricken, and the alternately dimming and brightening vision of *pacem in terris.* These, together with all of the added socio-spiritual confrontations which rack our society, are forcing our institutionalized forms of religion and communication toward deeper reappraisal of their activities and of the value of their participating in the lives of our citizens.

For it is certain that if we are to continue to hold our strength while bringing an often confused and weary populace toward some deeper sense of social and spiritual destiny, these institutions, above all others, must employ the new technology to bring the ancient dreams of mankind toward fulfillment. The growing recognition of this truth has led to a new kind of search. The churches and the broadcasters of America are now engaged in the quest for *relevance:* each to the individual, each to society, and each to the other.

We cannot, therefore, begin to examine the role of television in the religious life of our nation without first considering the entire spectrum of issues each must face, as well as the complex inter-relationships which have evolved within our religious and broadcast institutions. It is essential to consider the ways in which each is addressing itself to man at this time and place; and once having established the sensibilities and actions of each, it is of value to review the manner in which they have established a common bond of interest, overcome many of their differences, and engaged in the common quest for relevance. The purpose of the first section of this volume is to present a tentative exploration of these considerations.

Relevance: Church to Society, Broadcaster to Society

In a thoughtful overview of the current popularity of the term, Daniel Callahan notes that there are really three kinds of "relevance" sought by those who would bring fresh impact and contemporary appeal to the Christian message.

There is, above all, a significant pre-occupation with *theological* relevance—a concern which lies at the root of ancillary drives toward both *institutional* and *social* relevance. The concern for the intelligibility of the religious message is pervasive. Perhaps it is due to in Callahan's words[1] "a growing gulf between the traditional Orthodox supernaturalism in which our faith has been framed and the categories which the lay world (for want of a better term) finds meaningful today."

This deeper concern has inspired a current debate among theologians and theological philosophers which at some points moves to the fundamental level of questioning whether contemporary man can even experience the existence of God within any traditional framework of classical images of Creator and Creation. Thomas J. J. Altizer, Paul Van Buren, Gabriel Vahanian and others have spearheaded a "God-is-Dead" movement which (as the shock-value of the phrase testifies), expresses a bold attempt to find fresh language and concepts for traditional doctrine—for greater moral, liturgical, spiritual and theological relevance. If not all religious philosophers necessarily embrace the preoccupation of theology with relevance, the need of the churches to relate their own theological history to contemporary society still plays a dominant role in contemporary Christian and Jewish theological argument.

Several recent opinion studies reveal the causes for this concern. Unquestionably, one of the major issues facing modern religion is the prevalence of a belief that the church is losing its relevance to today's world. A Gallup Poll published in April, 1968 revealed that a majority of Americans today—67 per cent—say religion is "losing" its influence on American life. Exactly ten years ago the proportion holding this view was only one-fourth as large—14 per cent. This represents, according to the Gallup organization, a dramatic shift in American public opinion. The trend, it is concluded, has been steadily toward greater pessimism, and the altering view on the influence of religion has been accompanied by a decline in the proportion of persons who attend church in a typical week—from 49 per cent of the adult population in 1958 to 44 per cent in 1967.

Nor is this change exclusively American. A similar poll made

[1] Daniel Callahan, "The Quest for Social Relevance," *Daedelus* (Winter, 1967), p. 151.

in England in 1964 by the ABC Gallup research organization revealed that religion in the churches "plays little part in the lives of the vast majority of people," and that from many points of view religion is in decline. The study also reproduced some of the questions which had previously been employed in a 1957 British survey, and the report revealed that over the intervening years church-going dropped from 14 per cent of the population to ten per cent—a startling decrease in seven years. According to E. W. Whitley, head of research for Britain's ABC Television, there is ample evidence that religion *in the churches* does not seem important in people's lives. The number being confirmed appears to be declining. Forty-five per cent of the population think that religion is "old-fashioned" and "out of date" in relation to today's problems—an 18 per cent rise since 1957. Ninety-five per cent do not think church-going is "necessary for a good and useful life." Sixty-five per cent think other people's opinions have more influence on an individual's behavior than does religion. The lack of interest in formal religion is particularly strong among the young.

The British study is useful in setting forth some of the paradoxes which are involved in the quest for theological relevance. There is evidence, for example, of much individual belief and a very strong current of "friendly attitudes" toward religion. (Eighty-five per cent believe in God and only two per cent categorically do not. Sixty-four per cent believe Christ was the Son of God and fifty per cent believe in a life after death.) We may observe, then, a society well disposed towards religion, but little involved with it. In light of this paradox, and of what is undoubtedly a potentially similar situation in America, it is more than clear why the churches are in ferment, and why religious thought is so pre-occupied with theological relevance.

The Protestant theological historian Martin E. Marty[2] has described the second kind of concern which engages those who would speak through the religious experience to the situations of 20th century man—the search for relevance among religious insti-

2 Martin E. Marty, *Second Chance for American Protestants* (New York, Harper, 1963), p. 65.

tutions *qua* institutions. "The massive silhouette the churches (Catholic as well as Protestant) create on the American skyline is that of a self-preservative institutionalism," writes Marty ". . . the clergyman exists as a promoter of the organization . . . since the institutional self-interest pre-occupies the churches and does not directly serve the community, it seems to incarnate irrelevance."

The message from numerous thoughtful and concerned theologians is that there is a desperate need for religious institutions to go beyond the matters of organization and a pre-occupation with internal affairs and address themselves to genuine human needs. Some decry the reduction of Christianity to the dimensions of "a religious cult." Others lament the churches' lack of missionary zeal. The late Joseph Cardinal Ritter of St. Louis was concerned that Roman Catholicism is not presenting to youth a "sufficiently dramatic and meaningful church to engage their dedication to a life of sacrifice and service."

It is natural that the quest for institutional relevance also becomes a growing, vital, and widespread search for social relevance, for the two cannot, in fact, exist independently. "The essence of democracy," Jacques Maritain has written, "is evangelism, and its motive power is love." For many who share his view, it has become essential that religion move to make active and certain contributions to the secular commonweal.

In this phase of the quest for relevance the churches have been indicted for their failure to respond effectively to broad areas of contemporary social concern. Writes Margaret Mead, "Christian institutions continue to follow an inappropriate, inadequate and no longer relevant style of individual Christian charity. In doing so, they surrender to the secular world . . . the wider goals of feeding the hungry, caring for the sick and protecting the poor." [3]

The cry for social relevance within the churches has produced crises of leadership within religious institutions. Church leaders are accused of failing to "lead rather than follow" on vital social issues. A restless and active movement of the *engagés* among both clergy and laity has challenged institutionalized leadership, in-

[3] Margaret Mead, in Hugh C. White, Jr., ed., *Christians in a Technological Era* (New York, Seabury, 1964), p. 17.

spiring in turn opposition among those who resist the "secularizing" of theology—many of them hardly reactionary. Church leadership in larger established structures has willy-nilly been led into uneasy compromise, and on occasion been forced to discipline activist young clergy or to make religio-political decisions which have only fanned the flames.

Taken together, notes Callahan,[4] these crises and new conflicts are a "source of considerable pathos . . . On the most human level almost every church these days has its bewildered, sometimes panic-stricken members." The impact of his observation is brought home to anyone who has seen *A Time For Burning*— William Jersey's exciting 1966 film made for Lutheran Film Associates. This *verité* study of what happened to the congregation of a mid-western church when the issue of racial integration was introduced by its young minister bears witness to the dilemmas which face religion and the church in the second half of this century. The unhappy and uneasy division within this small congregation can be writ large across the face of American religion today —on all matters of theological, institutional and social relevance.

Yet it must be observed that the great dialogue has begun in those places which, by design and of necessity, still retain an interest in the whole man. It is the role of religion, Callahan concludes, to satisfy man's great spiritual hunger, and so long as it seeks to illuminate the human situation the quest for relevance cannot be abandoned. That relevance exists when the churches point to the existence of human needs in society, "when they try to take steps to alleviate these needs, *especially in conjunction with other groups* (italics mine), and when they work to preserve the idea of human dignity and justice."

No more significant point can be raised with reference to the role of television in its own quest for relevance, and it is well to review at this point the challenge to the American broadcaster, who is no less obliged to engage in his own search for identity and direction in a confused and complex age. He too must search for the means and methods by which to build a more meaningful existence for his fellow citizens. It has, of course, become habit for a few to insist that, because he operates within a framework

4 Callahan, op. cit., pp. 151–179.

which has admitted commerce as an important element within his system of values and judgments, the broadcaster cannot be effective. In light of the massive contributions which broadcasting has made to the entire society, such contentions can be dismissed as unrealistic in premise and untrue in fact. What is germane is whether broadcasting, along with all like institutions within our society, is capable of performing with integrity, dignity, and in full recognition of the needs of the society. The evidence argues overwhelmingly in the broadcasters' behalf.

Yet, they are challenged, constantly and correctly, to "do more and keep doing more" to speak to the situation of man, and here there are some obvious parallels between broadcasters and churchmen in American society. The efforts of both have endured criticism which reflects endless variations upon Martin E. Marty's theme[5] of irrelevance incarnate. Both have been blamed for failure of leadership. Both, in some eyes, stand as representatives of "establishment" institutions which could produce overnight a miraculous transformation of mankind but have refused to engage in the task. The telecaster, in particular, is believed to enjoy massive control of a society's attention, and statistical evidence (of the kind which demonstrates that people feel the church is losing its force in our society) is also summoned to prove that television is steadily gaining force in our society and "had better do something about it." In light of the bewilderment which these challenges must produce for the broadcaster, it is useful to survey his search for relevance to contemporary man within Callahan's framework[6] for the struggle toward religious relevance.

There is, quite clearly, a broadcaster's version of "theological" relevance. His mission, as established in his own conscience, is no less than to address the spirit of contemporary man; to inform and enlighten and by so doing to change, to influence and, hopefully, to inspire and energize. Yet the methods which are commended to him are precisely the opposite of those established by people who challenge our religious institutions. The broadcaster is under no compulsion whatever to modernize his "scripture,"

[5] Marty, op. cit., p. 65.
[6] Callahan, op. cit., pp. 151–179.

for his power was built, and indeed can only be sustained, by broad appeal to large audiences. The broadcaster's genius is to move goods and ideas quickly and efficiently by virtue of a communicative style which is at once dynamic and familiar with the idiom of large numbers of human souls. He has the American "beat."

Still he is asked to abandon or modify the style of his presentation—to avoid seeking great numbers, to limit the popularity of his messages, and consciously to serve "minority" audiences. It is a capital irony that while churches are challenged to make their messages significant to man by moving them into a broad and popular contemporary idiom, the broadcaster is asked to abandon or alter that idiom for the sake of presenting a more "significant" message. To this demand, the broadcaster has responded just as the church has responded—by holding his institutional base secure and extending probes in the form of increasing numbers of programs which vivify and dramatize the social issues of our time.

In this rough give-and-take of ideas between activists and traditionalists, both churchmen and broadcasters have learned that some giving is in order. The constant tension between individual and institution is part of the American broadcaster's sufferance, and the charge to him is made even more stringent by the interest, if not the threat, posed by regulative agencies representing the Federal Government, where occasional alarums and excursions by public servants will confuse as often as clarify, and build roadblocks as well as bridges.

Finally, the broadcaster is increasingly conscious of the fact that every move he makes has widespread, though immeasurable, social influence and impact. Unlike the churchman, however, the broadcaster in quest of social relevance is more often scorned for what he *is* doing rather than for what he fails to do. He operates in the classic do-and-be-damned-don't-and-be-damned mode. He is encouraged to editorialize—to have the courage to ignore "pressure" and to lead, and at the same time asked to be "fair" to all points of view. He is asked to reflect the political life of our society, and then condemned for turning politics into a "show." He is asked to set forth the raw and real confrontations of our time, and then flayed for "creating demagogues" and "sensation-alizing" his reports of our social ills and conflicts. He is asked to entertain and delight—to lift, with laughter and escape, the bur-dens of a tired and driven society and he is as promptly castigated for not being "serious." He is asked to help in building the eco-nomic base for a "great society" (where—in a reversal of histori-cal pattern—man must consume in order that he may work), and then is berated for creating "a nation of mass-consumption"—the prelude to some dire and dismal state of "mass-mindedness" in which it is but a short step from buying shaving cream to blind acceptance of some charismatic (and evil) political leader.

This is the dilemma which confronts the broadcaster as he seeks to make his institution socially relevant, and it is fair to observe that the demands which are put upon him are as right as they are wrong. He has little choice but to heed each new criti-cism in turn and attempt to answer those which his professional instinct tells him are true and accurate. He has come, with reluc-tance, to accept the truth of Paul Ylvisaker's words,[7] ". . . as long as America's broadcasters can see bricks being thrown at them from every side, they can be sure they are not far from the place where they are needed." But with this acceptance the American broadcaster is coming of age. By struggling to fit his own sense of responsibility into the communicative system he controls; by blending the essential interests of government, commerce, educa-tion and the complex of institutions serving man's spiritual and creative needs, the broadcaster too has begun to speak of the con-dition of man.

There is, then, no easy path toward relevance for either broad-casting or religion. Both exist as essential institutions which must mediate between what needs to be done and what, at this time and in these circumstances, can be done. To abandon the insti-tutional character of either is unthinkable, and to anticipate that they may move in any direction without a considerable degree of institutional power, independence and authority is fanciful, if not anarchistic. The best we may expect perhaps, is "Vice-

[7] Paul Ylvisaker, "Conscience and the Community," *TV Quarterly* (Winter, 1964), p. 14.

Presidents (and Bishops) In Charge of Anarchy." Herein may lie
one significant hope for making the message of church and broadcaster relevant in our time.

Relevance: The Broadcaster to Religion, Religion to the Broadcaster

The kind of cooperation between television and our religious
institutions which is detailed in this volume is not a phenomenon
of recent years. American broadcasters have enjoyed a long and
generally amiable relationship with the religious agencies and organizations which, since the earliest days of radio, sensed the
unique contributions which electronic communication could
offer in service of their mission. It would be misleading, however, to say that the relationship, historically and in this decade,
has been altogether without friction. The urgencies of mission
and religious zeal, on the one hand, and the realities of commercial broadcasting and audience behavior, on the other, have produced continuing debate and discussion on the role of TV and
radio in American religious life. Such differences between broadcaster and religious institutions have been attentuated by a continuing argument within the churches themselves over the proper
uses of the broadcast media.

In the dialogue between church and broadcasting, the principal concerns of the broadcaster are: (1) What policies should he
adopt regarding the assignment of air time to the multiplicity of
different religious groups and organizations? and (2) Beyond his
own recognition of community religious needs, what is required
of him by law and by regulative directive? In neither of these
aspects of his day-to-day decision-making are the answers clear,
and operators of TV and radio stations are fully aware that errors
in judgment may create severe difficulties for them.

The broadcaster's concern over the assignment of time to various groups and denominations, for example, has in part arisen
out of a history of unhappy situations resulting from use of his
facilities by "splinter" religious organizations. These have often
led the broadcaster into those gray areas where his legal as well as

moral responsibilities to the greater community are open to question. In an April, 1967 report for *TV Guide,* Neil Hickey estimated that some 10,000 weekly programs which have been identified as outlets for spokesmen of "the radical right" are broadcast in the United States—primarily on radio. To the chagrin and regret of responsible religious institutions and agencies, many of these broadcasts are identified as "religious," even though, as Hickey reported, "Fear is indeed their most important product, as well as hatred, suspicion and a fine sense of conspiracy." Among the best-known groups which carry a fiery religious and political fundamentalism to audiences are *The Christian Crusade,* operated by the Reverend Dr. Billy James Hargis of Tulsa, Oklahoma, and *The 20th Century Reformation Hour,* an outlet for the Reverend Carl McIntire, who was expelled from the Presbyterian Church in 1936 for causing "dissension and strife" and generating "suspicion and ill will." The "religious" connotation unfortunately often associated with such programs poses a common concern for responsible religious groups as well as station operators.

The FCC's "Fairness Doctrine" cannot be brought to bear upon the question until citizen complaints are received, and the agency likewise cannot monitor the thousands of such broadcasts to determine whether a station should be required to grant free time for reply to an individual or organization which has been attacked. In any case, broadcasters who seek governmental assistance in such matters tend to feel that they are sailing between Scylla and Charybdis. For many broadcasters, seeking application of the "Fairness Doctrine" in an area of socio-political concern where it would be convenient to let others make decisions may only lead to increased regulative activity in other areas where broadcasters feel they alone should carry responsibility.

Confronted with this problem, the broadcaster's natural inclination is to resist encroachment upon his own rights and responsibilities by developing working relationships only with recognized and established religious groups. The wider the community he serves, the more broad and inclusive are the organizations whose support he seeks, and this practice has created some differences of opinion between broadcasters and churchmen. In most larger communities there are organized councils of churches that represent the major faith groups, and so broadcasters deal mainly with Catholics, Protestants and Jews. Nevertheless, there are numerous denominations that do not participate in councils of churches, ranging in size from the very large Southern Baptist Church down to very small sects.

Even when the broadcaster recognizes the significant need for serving smaller religious groups, the possibility of irresponsible actions by charlatans who use religion as a mask for anti-social activity has made him wary; and if he can overcome this wariness, he is still confronted with the problems created when a great number of groups come to him for air time on an independent basis. He has learned that such an approach may be self-defeating from both his and their point of view. As the number of spokesmen grows, the impact of each individual effort will lessen in proportion—for a variety of reasons ranging from the plethora of religious messages on the air to the scattering of that creative energy and force which meaningful programming so desperately requires. Hence the broadcaster's tendency to concentrate forces.

But if the broadcaster can face with confidence the need to create an intelligent and progressive balance between the forces who would enlarge his freedom and those who would restrict it, both he and the religious organizations seeking wider use of radio and television for the spiritual growth of man must also deal with a new and more dramatic issue—the very legality of their right to do so.

From the beginning of broadcasting, the Federal Communications Commission (and before it, the Federal Radio Commission) has stipulated in a variety of ways that the broadcaster must recognize the role of religion in the community and plan his program service in such a manner as to reflect religious interests. Broadcasters have responded dutifully over the years to such requirements. But they are now confronted with the possibility that the Commission's requirements in this regard may be unconstitutional, and that efforts in religious programming now under way may in fact be in violation of the law of the land.

In early 1965 communications-lawyer Marcus Cohn[8] claimed that the Federal Communications Commission has "been doing its best to get people to go to church" as a result of its requirement for a listing of times and amount of religious programming on license-renewal forms. Cohn charged that the weight placed on religious programming is a "heavy factor" in reviewing renewal applications, and cited three licensing examples of attention paid to religious programming. While Cohn found no specific evidence that religious programming proposals are the sole deciding factor in licensing, he noted that the FCC has, for example, "implicitly, though not explicitly, found sponsored religious programming inferior to sustaining," and further observed that the Federal Communications Commission license application singles out the religious category by demanding an indication of whether the projected programming is sponsored or sustaining, but did not require the same information in other programming categories.

Observing that it is one thing for the FCC to require ascertainment of the educational and agricultural needs of the community but quite another for the FCC to require a judgment of the religious needs of the community, Cohn concluded that "it is quite clear that the mere existence of the question on the application form compels the applicant to commit himself to foster the practice and growth of religion."

This position might not have had such impact had not a member of the Federal Communications Commission supported the argument. In a lengthy discussion of broadcasting and religious liberty first published in the *George Washington Law Review,* Commissioner Lee Loevinger[9] reviewed the entire history of court actions regarding religious liberty and questioned whether the FCC has not rushed in "where government agencies are forbidden to tread." Loevinger noted that in a number of reported cases the Commission has required religious programming and

---

[8] Marcus Cohn, "Religion and the FCC," *The Reporter* (Jan. 14, 1965), pp. 32–34.

[9] Lee Loevinger, speech to National Religious Broadcasters, Jan. 27, 1965, *George Washington Law Review,* Vol. 33 (March, 1965), p. 631.

determined that a certain amount of religious broadcasting is or is not adequate or excessive; decreed that the public interest is or is not served by the broadcasting of particular views on religion or of the views or particular churches or sects; and awarded preference or demerit to applicants on the basis of official judgment as to the quantity, quality or content of religious broadcasting.

"All commentators," said Loevinger, "agree that both the words and principles of the Supreme Court decisions in this field warn government agencies against any intrusions into the area of religion." To Loevinger, the plain and unavoidable duty of the Commission is to follow the letter and spirit of the law as declared by the Constitution, enacted by Congress and interpreted by the Supreme Court. In response to such protestations, former FCC Chairman E. William Henry answered that the Commission "welcomed" such debate if it would help both regulator and regulated to arrive at steady and consistent standards for judging broadcast performance.

Whether such debate will ever be resolved is an academic question, for the fact is that if the broadcaster involves himself with the religious institutions of his community it is because he recognizes instinctively that such involvement is essential for him to perform in the public interest. The broadcaster who carries religious programs and involves himself in the religious life of his community does so because he is conscious of the public need, and it is a small comfort to him and to those who wish to make use of the airwaves for such purposes to sense that legal and regulative confusions seem to abound in the matter.

The principal concerns of representatives of religious institutions who wish to make use of the airwaves are: (1) How can they reconcile the debate within their ranks over secularization of religion through the mass media? and (2) How can they reduce the argument among their own agencies regarding the role which the Federal Government should play in religious broadcasting activities?

Clearly the churches and faith-groups of America must come to terms with larger questions of the appropriateness of their involvement in mass media. There is disagreement over the entire approach of religion in broadcasting—a conflict which stems from theological concern over what is termed the "growing secularization of religion." Earnest men have spoken out on both sides of the issue, and their basic differences of opinion regarding an approach to man in a "new idiom" must produce some misgivings among those who wish to blend the religious message and the mass media modes of communication.

Martin E. Marty has argued, for instance, that the greater threat to the Christian faith in today's communications come not from the secularist, but from the religionist himself—"precisely because the religionist, the last person who should do so, often succumbs to the gimmicks and the jargon and thereby isolates faith behind barriers of blandness." Marty's view is echoed by John G. Deedy, Jr., who, in an essay titled "Madison Avenue Religion," cautioned the "professional peddler" against selling religion "as if it were cold beer or Fuller Brushes." "The promoting of religion," wrote Deedy, "has always been a challenge, and over the centuries some terrifying sins have been committed under that heading." For Deedy, "the soft sell of a Bishop Sheen or a Billy Graham" might assure that the already saved are made more secure in their faith, "but we suspect that it hardens the heretic in the same way as do billboard signs that one day proclaim 'Bosco is Good For You,' and the next 'The Family That Prays Together, Stays Together.' "

Many openly dispute such attitudes. Reflecting the sentiments of many media activists, an Episcopal priest, The Reverend John P. Davidson, has written:

> Television demands a new dimension in its use which we have not begun to discover. Industry has discovered much about modern communication and is well along in developing its use. We have only to think back to last night's television and recall the impact of advertising for Black Label, for example, or "Coke," or Tiparillo—or the impact on our thinking and knowledge that Walter Cronkite or the Huntley-Brinkley report has. Education is pouring billions into the more effective use of electronic media in our electronically-conditioned culture. I believe the church must do the same.

Davidson's argument reflects a belief held by many of various faiths who argue in defense of a more pragmatic and realistic approach to the use of broadcasting's capacities to engage the wider audience. Father James Brown, chairman of the Radio-TV department at the University of Detroit, has urged that the churches drop the traditional methods of presenting religious thought on television. Paul M. Stevens, director of the Radio and Television Commission of the Southern Baptist Convention, has defended the pace and excitement of commercial programming in religious presentations. "Religious programming," wrote Stevens, "does not need any special coddling. It thrives best in a normal atmosphere of the work-a-day world. It needs no insulation from normal programming—no separation for any reason."

This dialogue within the ranks of religious institutions must obviously have influence upon how they engage the services of broadcasting. The dilemma posed is the need to be effective on broadcasting's terms as well as on religious terms. As religious institutions relate to the broadcaster they must be prepared to enter into a state of give-and-take in which there are no categorical imperatives of approach and method other than those of taste, imagination and inventive artistry consistent with the objective to reach and affect an audience.

The second principal concern of the religious programmer is closely identified with the broadcaster's quest for realistic and consistent regulative policy. Among churchmen there is some division of opinion regarding the role which the Federal Communications Commission should play in their broadcasting activities. Many have called for more active FCC involvement, insisting that the Commission force broadcasters to grant more and better broadcast time to churches, while many others have argued that the opposite is far more suitable.

In an essay published in *The Christian Century*, Desmond Smith[10] deprecated the contributions of broadcasters and insisted that "churches cannot remain silent. Their choice is not one of politics (government control of television) but one of policies: in

[10] Desmond Smith, "Churches and the Airwaves," *The Christian Century* (Mar. 24, 1965), p. 367.

favor of or against an activist Christian concern with every aspect of broadcasting. Only by such commitment can Christianity, in this Christian nation, get a foothold in the television industry where currently it hangs on by bruised fingernails." A different view is expressed by Theodore F. Lott,[11] as published in *The Beam.* "We rebel at the thought of government's telling broadcasters they must broadcast religion," he writes, ". . . and with sufficient time allocation to satisfy the government. The broadcast industry has taken care of that in both the radio and television codes. And we, as a religious production agency, have fared well at the industry's hand. We have been treated so generously we could not translate our gratitude into words."

A more mediating view seems to be in evidence, however, as both parties to the debate come to recognize that the amount of time extended by broadcasters is related inevitably to the capacities of the message to attract audience response. The religious programmer has begun to share responsibility with the broadcaster, perhaps under the stimulation of such critical observations as recorded by Jack Gould [12] in the *New York Times:* "If the church feels unjustly relegated to a ghetto in broadcast schedules, it must ask itself whether it should not accept at least part of the responsibility, whether the scope of its activities and the reality of its participation in everyday life does not invite such a circumscribed hearing. The answer may lie more in what the church does off the air than on."

The broadcaster, too, has been rebuked, to the point of public embarrassment in such proceedings as the FCC's 1962 Chicago hearings[13] into the scope of community involvement by broadcasters—an ill-advised kind of "hanging trial" which may have done more to estrange those forces already working in collective harmony than to bring them closer together. But beyond this kind of unnecessary Federal prodding, there is little doubt that some broadcasters deserve sharp criticism for past failures to encourage more forceful and energetic religious effort in their communities.

11 Theodore F. Lott, "Religion on the Air," *The Beam* (Aug., 1965), p. 27.
12 Jack Gould, *The New York Times* (July 19, 1964), Sec. II, p. 13.
13 FCC Hearings, Chicago, 1962. See *Broadcasting* (Apr. 2, 9, 16 and 23, 1962).

The past cannot be changed but it can be instructive. It is proper to observe that we are now witnessing a new and meaningful evolution of religious broadcasting in America—a development stimulated by the efforts of those broadcasters and religious agencies who have long been engaged in the task of creating programs, and are now influencing others to begin to use the electronic media in forceful and creative ways. The subsequent sections of this volume demonstrate that a common goal is in view and that the deeds are beginning to outrun the differences.

. . . *A mass society has come into being which, through these instruments, has given itself a mass culture. The intellectual is contemptuous of it and rejects it, but the fact remains that this mass culture contains real human values: a thirst for knowledge and truth, a need to communicate these with every means and with all speed so that men may be in communication with each other, and finally a cultural heritage accessible to all and offered as a gift. These values must find their own theological interpretation so that a new humanism can be realized.*

Archbishop Andrea Pangrazio
—quoted in *Ave Maria,* National
Catholic Weekly, January 2, 1965.

THE MARK OF CAIN, John Butler ballet (above), was commissioned for CBS-TV's *Lamp Unto My Feet*. Carmen de Lavallade danced the role of Eve. An Evening of Afro-American Prose and Poetry, by the Free Southern Theater, was adapted for a telecast of the CBS's *Look Up and Live* (below).

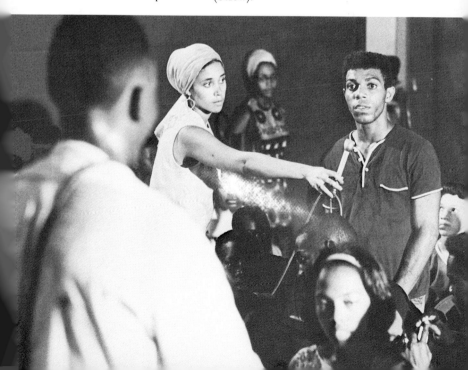

EYES UPON THE CROSS (left) dramatized a biblical story. It was produced by KOCO-TV, Oklahoma City. A network-originated drama was "I Never Saw Another Butterfly." The NBC-TV *Eternal Light* production dealt with the tragedy of the Terezin concentration camp (below).

DRAMATIC CHALLENGE: Marian Seldes portrayed three different women who lived at the turn of the century—Emma Lazarus, Lillian Wald and Hannah Solomon (l. to r.)—on one telecast of ABC-TV's *Directions*, "Three Women."

Another *Directions* telecast provocatively conceived and titled was the drama-satire, "Will The Real Jesus Christ Please Stand Up?" (below). The program was later bought by England's BBC.

FILMS: One of the most popular religious series distributed to local television stations is the Lutheran Church's *Davey and Goliath* (above), which has strong appeal for young audiences. *The Vine* (below, left) is an hour-long special, produced by NBC and the Radio & Television Commission of the Southern Baptist Convention. A program series distributed by the National Council of Churches was *Talkback* (below, right), produced by the Methodist Television, Radio & Film Commission.

Guaranteed
Safety
for
100
YEARS

RELIGIOUS MUSICAL PROGRAMS are offered by many local stations. *Sermons in Song* (above) is a presentation of KIII, Corpus Christi, Texas. *The Singing Nuns* are seen on WTHI-TV, Terre Haute, Indiana.

SISTERS of Our Lady of Victory work on WTEV's *The Little Flock* (above, left) in New Bedford, Mass. Dramatic effects spark young imaginations on WBBM-TV's *The Magic Door* (above, right), Chicago. *Kumzitz,* also produced by the Chicago Board of Rabbis, is "an entertaining learning experience."

ECUMENICAL APPROACH is typified by *The Challenge Panel* on KOMO-TV, Seattle, with Father William Treacy, Rabbi Raphael Levine and Dr. Lynn Corson. Adventure is incorporated in *By Gemini*. Produced by the Catholic Archdiocese of Chicago, it features a "space priest" and a young girl.

QUILTING BEE: "Keep in Circulation the Rumor that God is Alive" is a scene from a film spot distributed by the National Council of Churches. The Council's programs included *Breakthru,* which on one telecast starred Anne Ives and Patty Duke. The Council also used a spot of boys playing (below, right) to convey the message "God cares."

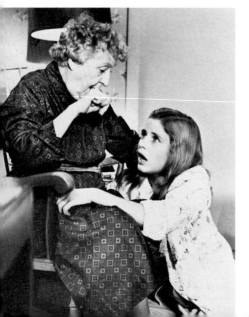

II

RELIGIOUS TELEVISION
PROGRAMMING IN
AMERICA

DESPITE THE CONFLICTS which both churches and television must experience, there is, in fact, a great deal of religious programming. Even as the deeper questions of philosophy and approach are posed, the religious program specialist and the telecaster must still deal with the day-to-day matters of formulating policy and presenting programs. The questions now become more direct: What is being done? What needs to be done? In light of what we know, what is the best way to go about doing it? And, once some firm criteria are established in these areas, how can they be extended to others? It was in this spirit that the Television Information Office commissioned the present study (the third in a series of program surveys it has developed), which is designed to produce direct and meaningful information concerning the scope and nature of religious television programming at the community level in America.

As in the earlier studies of this type (*Interaction* and *For the Young Viewer*), those programs which receive more detailed description below are randomly selected, and no inferences of comparative value should be assigned those given greater space in description, those briefly described and those merely listed. A governing factor in the selection of a program for more lengthy description was the degree of representativeness it seemed to hold for a larger class of similar programs, not a judgment of its qualitative superiority to others within that class.

Again as in earlier surveys, the study motivation is tri-fold. First and foremost, it is of considerable value for telecaster and religious program specialist alike to extend their own awareness of what others are doing in the field. Such a survey can identify program ideas, production approaches and studio techniques which may stimulate further innovation and freshness in conceptualization for those who are caught up in a very natural "forest-and-tree" pattern. Thus, the fresh view on creative programming and production is a value unto itself.

Next, the survey is designed to attract the attention of many who are not now engaged in such effort. The scope and intensity of the broad effort described herein may serve to underscore Wilbur Schramm's observation that more non-professional members of the public must learn to use the media. "There is no excuse for religious broadcasting being less skillful than entertainment broadcasting," wrote Schramm, "and for leaders of any community to acquire the basic skills of broadcasting would not be a great task." Nor is there, it may be added, any excuse for the telecaster who does not seek to promote such involvement in his community. Such a survey as reported here, then, may serve to stimulate interest and professional involvement where it did not before exist.

Finally, there is the equally valuable motivation to inform the general public of an activity by telecasters which reflects their commitment to the public interest. Catch-phrases and slogans so casually applied to TV in the print media may, with good cause, rankle the telecaster who feels that his efforts go unrecognized. It is a good thing when he can present his genuine accomplishments in this more permanent form, where they can be examined and considered by the public to whom he is executing his responsibility.

Study Procedures and Results

The survey reported here is based upon responses to a detailed questionnaire which was sent to all TV stations in the U.S.A. in 1966. Stations were asked to provide specific information concerning their religious program activity during the year July 1, 1964 to June 30, 1965, as well as to enter descriptions of their own locally-created programs. In addition to quantitative information about such matters as the number of hours of programs carried each week, the questionnaire also sought qualitative information regarding program types and styles, and the subjective evaluations of the value and professional quality of programs which the station aired. Effort was also made to discover those factors which TV decision-makers took into account when assigning time for religious programs.

Over 430 individual stations responded to the survey. These represented a fairly even distribution in network affiliation—140 ABC-TV, 147 CBS-TV, 138 NBC-TV. Twenty-two unaffiliated stations responded, as did 54 educational television stations. The typical responding station was found to carry approximately two hours of religious programming each week, of which 60 minutes was in the form of syndicated programs, 30 minutes in network offerings and 30 minutes locally-originated. Adding the production costs and the rate-card value of station time, the dollars committed by the 250 stations reporting financial data in this survey would total over $1,200,000 each week, or an average of slightly more than $5,000 per station in each week of the survey year.

The survey revealed that most stations seemed to regard syndicated programs as more important than network offerings. In their program evaluations of local and syndicated material, the stations considered most programs which they aired as "good," and the next greatest number of evaluations termed the programs "excellent." Many programs were considered "fair" and very few were regarded as "poor."

In response to a query concerning those factors which determine the time in which religious programs are scheduled, most stations indicated that the quality of the program was the most important criterion in assigning schedule time. The next most important factor listed was station policy on religious time, and the third most frequently mentioned factor was "probability of attracting intended audience." The desires of the program's sponsor was given a very low priority in this matter.

As a result of this survey it is easy to conclude that religious programming is a significant aspect of local television in America. A great many programs are being carried, and there is firm indication of growing interest in religious programming. Yet it is also clear that there is a strong tendency for the local stations to look to the larger program-producing organizations—networks and religious groups—for the bulk of religious programming they carry. Thus it is necessary, before turning to the descriptions of local efforts, to consider in some detail the role of these agencies, for in their work may be found the keys to a still greater and more meaningful local programming effort.

Syndicated and Network Religious Programmings

"It's a bit of a secret. Only those people who on Sunday are neither in church nor asleep nor buried in the papers know it: religious TV is more varied, skilled, sophisticated and imaginative then ever before."

So wrote a *Time*[1] observer in the lead paragraph of a brief overview of religious television written shortly after the conclusion of the telecasting season reviewed here. The briefest examination of syndicated and network offerings in that season confirms the anonymous opinion. What emerges from such analysis is the clear fact that syndicators, network program units and the faith-group advisory bodies with which they work have moved with alacrity to employ the contemporary idiom in speaking to the condition of man.

The local station turns to these national sources of religious programming for the same reasons that it relies upon networks

1 "Excitement on the Tube," *Time* (Jan. 28, 1966), p. 70.

and program syndication companies for cultural, entertainment and public affairs programs. Station groups (e.g., Westinghouse and Corinthian), because they operate upon a wider financial base, will produce more interesting and better prepared programs. To be sure, there are many instances where the local station can provide programs which are conceived and produced with as much verve and genuine creative spirit as any of the great network and syndicator offerings. Still, one would anticipate that the concentration of forces in national-level programming would enable the production of superior work. A national organization can more easily attract major performers, writers and other creative personnel. It can afford more lavish production. The typical local station would be hard pressed to produce a major panel discussion featuring leading theologians and religious leaders of the nation, and it is rarely possible for even the largest of local TV stations to commission an independent production of a complete opera or produce a full series of well-staged dramas. Yet these are regular offerings by network religious program units and larger syndicating organizations.

Syndication Activity

Over a score of organizations and agencies are now engaged in the design, production and distribution of religious programs for both network and local radio and TV stations in America. A number of these maintain active production units. Others commission programs to be made by independent production agencies with their advice and consultation and still others offer regular consultation services for network and station programming.

The major faith-groups in the United States—Protestant, Catholic and Jewish—have each established organizations to serve their aims in utilization of the mass media. The National Council of Churches of Christ in the U.S.A. maintains the Broadcasting and Film Commission, which represents 18 Protestant denominations in the United States, who in turn maintain units and offices for the specific purpose of media utilization. The Roman Catholic Church was served by two major groups—the

National Council of Catholic Men, which produced programs in cooperation with the three major networks in behalf of the American Catholic church, and the recently-established National Catholic Office for Radio and Television. The latter was created by the bishops in the United States in late 1965, following publication of the Vatican Council Pronouncement on Communications. Headed by the Most Reverend John A. Donovan, Bishop of Toledo, the NCORT is the official point of reference in the U.S. on all broadcast matters for both the Pontifical Commission on Social Communications and the Catholic International Association for Radio and Television. The Jewish Theological Seminary of America maintains an active Department of Radio and Television which is responsible for the supervision of the radio and television versions of *The Eternal Light* program as well as for cooperation in production of network programs dealing with the Jewish faith.

Protestant

The Broadcasting and Film Commission of the National Council of Churches of Christ in the United States, the largest and most widely representative of such organizations, was established in 1950 as a special body of the newly-formed NCC, and merged with the Protestant Film Commission and Protestant Radio Commission. Under the current direction of William F. Fore, BFC activities in TV have steadily expanded since it began TV work in the early 1950's. The Radio-TV units within various major denominations represented by the NCC work in active cooperation with the BFC, producing religious materials for TV in their own behalf and also assisting in BFC production. In 1964 and 1965 the BFC distributed six major program series on film to appproximately 232 TV stations in each year. These series contain from 13 to 39 programs each.

All of the denominational units within the BFC have been active in the service of local television throughout the United States, and it is possible here to give no more than brief treatment to the varied activities of a few of the more active agencies.

- The Commission on Press, Radio and Television, Lutheran Church in America, is responsible for one of the most popular children's programs in religious television, the *Davey and Goliath* series. Thirty-nine programs in this series, as well as a *Davey and Goliath* special, were offered to local audiences over many TV stations in the survey year. The series was consistently ranked by responding stations as "excellent." Another Lutheran denomination, the American Lutheran Church, offered TV spot announcements for syndication.

- The work of the Television, Radio and Film Commission (TRAFCO) of the Methodist Church was of equal significance in American TV during the survey year, and among the most widely-seen of its series was the 19-program series of children's programs, *Breakthru,* which is designed to foster deeper religious understanding through drama and discussion.

- *Faith For Today,* an independent program series sponsored by the General Conference of Seventh Day Adventists, was also widely viewed during the year. This series, emphasizing a broader "family" view with a practical rather than theological emphasis, was carried on 235 local TV stations in the survey year.

- The Division of Radio-TV of The United Presbyterian Church in the U.S.A. also offered free public service programming to local TV stations. Among the major efforts of the survey year was a 13-program series of half-hour documentary films, *Adventurous Mission.* The unit pioneered in the use of short forms of program for repetitive broadcast and is responsible for the "God is Alive" series of syndicated spot-announcements.

- The Office of Communication of the United Church of Christ offered to local TV stations a 13-program series, *Tangled World,* a unique course in ethics featuring Dr. Roger Shinn of Union Theological Seminary.

These barely suggest the range of syndicated drama, documentary, and discussion programs and series, as well as specials, spot announcements and related services and materials offered to local TV stations by the members of the BFC.

The efforts described above represent the great bulk of Protestant engagement in American TV, but additional program material is supplied by Protestant groups outside the National Council, including the Lutheran Church-Missouri Synod, which is a BFC observer but offers its own consultation and program services. Perhaps the most important of the programs this organization offers is *This is The Life,* a 30-minute dramatic series which has been seen on American TV for nearly 15 years, and was aired by over 375 stations in the U.S. and Canada during the survey year.

Certainly the largest of the independent Protestant program-producing units is maintained by the Southern Baptist Convention, whose Radio and Television Commission, under the direction of Dr. Paul M. Stevens, supports a million-dollar broadcasting center in Forth Worth, Texas. This unit produces approximately 200 radio and television programs a year, and among the TV programs offered free to local stations in the survey were such 30-minute color film series as *Mastercontrol, Patterns, The Baptist Hour* and *The Answer.* Perhaps the most widely heralded single program of the year in review was "The Inheritance," an hour-long recreation of biblical history produced by NBC-TV in cooperation with the Southern Baptist Convention (see Network Programming below).

Catholic

The Roman Catholic Church's National Catholic Office for Radio and Television, official information-consultation agency, in 1969 assumed responsibility for all regular network religious programs. Bishop John A. Donovan, of Toledo, is chairman, Charles E. Reilly, Jr., executive director. Independent Catholic agencies, e.g., St. Francis Productions, working with NCORT, provide syndicated series.

During the survey year, 441 Catholic programs were being

aired by local TV stations in the United States, and 123 foreign TV stations also carried such syndicated programs. The most widely-seen of these were Father James Keller's *The Christophers,* carried by 225 stations, *The Sacred Heart Hour,* aired by 115 local stations, and the Paulist Fathers' *Insight* series.

Jewish

In comments included in the survey, it was frequently noted that the Jewish faith has not yet made sufficient efforts to provide syndicated programs for local TV stations. Both the Jewish Theological Seminary of America and the New York Board of Rabbis have provided steady cooperation on network programming over the years, but there are as yet no large agencies serving the Jewish faith engaged in the production of the kind of syndicated programs and series offered by Protestant and Catholic organizations described above.

The mainstay series representing the Jewish faith in the American communities continues to be the NBC-TV network offering, *The Eternal Light,* produced for the Jewish Theological Seminary by Milton E. Krentz. Carried on over 100 TV stations throughout the nation, the televised version of *The Eternal Light* has a weekly audience of four million and receives over 4,000 letters each week. The Department of Radio and Television of the Jewish Theological Seminary has broadened its network program interests in recent years, and does attempt to supplement the network airing of *The Eternal Light* by making scripts available for interested parties. Kinescopes and films of certain of the programs are also made available by the National Academy for Adult Jewish Studies.

The above no more than touches upon the total range of syndicated religious programming made available to local television stations throughout the year in which this study was conducted. Nor does it enable the reader to judge the quality of individual programs and series which are offered to the American public in this way. It is presented merely to suggest the scope and organization of the religious programs in syndication for television. A judgment of quality implicit in the work described, however, is expressed by local TV station operators, who devote to these efforts, on the average, about one-half of all the air-time they assign to religious programs.

Network Activity

With many notable exceptions among the output of both syndicating and local units, it is fair to describe the efforts of the American networks in the field of religious programming as seminal. The dominant programming thrust of the networks, along with the potentiality for instantaneous national distribution, has quite naturally attracted the interests and efforts of those who wish to use television in service of religion. From the outset, the national faith organizations have developed strong working liaisons with network public affairs departments, who have in turn relied upon the major faith groups to offer advice, consultation, production assistance and, in some cases, completely produced programs. For a variety of reasons, the network programs have included many different genres, including experimental productions.

Each of the networks currently sustains weekly programs created and produced within their own organizations. The Public Affairs Department of ABC News offers the *Directions* series, produced by Wiley Hance. CBS-TV regularly offers two 30-minute series each Sunday, *Look Up and Live* and *Lamp Unto My Feet,* produced by the Religious Program Department headed by Pamela Ilott. At NBC-TV, Doris Ann directs the Religious Program Department of NBC News, which is responsible for production of a weekly telecast featuring three independent sub-series: *Frontiers of Faith, The Catholic Hour* and *The Eternal Light.*

Time on both CBS-TV and NBC-TV is divided roughly in proportion to the size of each of the major faith groups within the population (three Protestant, two Catholic, one Jewish), and at ABC-TV the ratio is equal. It is estimated that some 300 local affiliates of the combined networks clear time for these regularly-scheduled telecasts, and the Broadcasting and Film Commission of the National Council of Churches estimates that Protestant offerings alone in these network series are seen by some 1,500,000 viewers each week.

Historically, the ABC-TV *Directions* series had its origins in radio early in the decade, and entered its fifth season of telecasting during the year under examination. The two CBS-TV offerings, *Lamp Unto My Feet and Look Up And Live* were first started in 1948 and 1954, respectively, and the NBC-TV religious programs began some 15 years ago under the direction of Edward Stanley. There has, of course, been a long history of religious radio broadcasting by all networks.

ABC Television Network

Directions

Among the *Directions '65* programs produced in cooperation with the Jewish Theological Seminary was an original Passover Opera, "The Final Ingredient," based on a play by Reginald Rose which had been telecast in an earlier season. Commemorating the Jewish Festival of Freedom, the work dealt with the survival of an ancient spirit and tradition amidst the brutality and degradation of a Nazi concentration camp. Written by David Amram, who also conducted the ABC Symphony for the performance, "The Final Ingredient" was commissioned by ABC. Other programs representing the Jewish faith included a four-program series dealing with Jewish artists and writers, an award-winning film dealing with Chaim Weizmann, the scientist-statesman who became the first president of Israel, and a dramatic-form inquiry concerning the ancient Gods and the evolution of Judaic monotheism.

Programs representing the Catholic faith on *Directions '65* included examinations of urgent social issues as well as matters related to the changing church. Among the twelve programs produced with the cooperation of the National Council of Catholic Men were a film portrayal of "Synanon," the controversial Westport, Connecticut rehabilitation center for narcotics addicts, and a program devoted to the story of an emotionally-disturbed boy in which playwright Robert Cream re-created the boy's story as told by his own family. Other programs reflecting broader social concerns included "Racism and The American Catholic," which presented a discussion of the problems of racial prejudice featuring three Negro members of the Catholic clergy, and "Behold The Tears," a documentary which examined the Christian sources of Anti-Semitism. Among the programs created more specifically for viewers of the Catholic faith were an investigation of the music of worship for the new Catholic mass, followed by the telecasting of the reformed version of the mass—a project which earned for ABC-TV a Gabriel Award from the Catholic Broadcasters Association of America. These, together with memorial tributes to President Kennedy and writer Flannery O'Conner, constituted the Roman Catholic contribution to *Directions '65*.

The twelve Protestant programs in *Directions '65* were produced in conjunction with the National Council of Churches, the Southern Baptist Convention, and the United Presbyterian Church in the U.S.A. The Council cooperated in production of a five-program series, "The Mysteries of Life." ABC News correspondent Don Goddard was host for these programs which focused on the relationship between science and religion and on the challenging questions raised by science's new theories and accomplishments. Additional *Directions* efforts in association with Protestant organizations included "Forty-eight Hours With God," a program reviewing the current growing Protestant interest in religious retreats, "The Art of Stained Glass," an exploration of an art which had been lost for the past three hundred years and is again flourishing, and two Christmas programs. Patricia Morrison and John Riordan were star soloists in "Sing a Song for Christmas," an hour-long musical presentation, and "Who May Call This Family His Own?" presented the Nativity as interpreted and depicted by the folk painters and sculptors of many lands and cultures through the centuries.

Even though Producer Wiley Hance is adamant on the point that "a network must do something beyond the mere carrying of religious services," ABC-TV did carry certain traditional major services—the Christmas Eve Mass from the National Shrine of The Immaculate Conception in Washington, D.C. and the special Christmas Eve Services from the Cathedral of St. John The Divine (Protestant-Episcopal) in New York City—and also became the first network to telecast an Easter Vigil Service.

CBS Television Network

Look Up and Live

Since its inception over a decade ago, the CBS-TV *Look Up and Live* series has also worked in close cooperation with leading faith groups, and advisory arrangements have been established between the network's religious program unit and the Broadcasting and Film Commission of the National Council of Churches, the National Council of Catholic Men, and the New York Board of Rabbis. The advisory procedures resulted in a discernible pattern in *Look Up and Live* programming already observed in such sub-series as "The Mysteries of Life" at ABC-TV; that is, mutual planning efforts led to the creation of shorter series of several programs which in turn allowed for a deeper investigation of a major aspect of religious faith.

Thus the National Council of Churches cooperated in the eight-program "Image of Man" series, which presented an overview of man as currently reflected in significant productions of the stage, films, television and contemporary music. Additional series developed from Protestant sources in the season under review included the four-program "Power, Person and The Gospel," and "A Common Calling," a four-program analysis of the search for unity by modern-day American Protestantism. The Reverend Harvey Cox served as host for a two-program drama-discussion entitled "A Question of Identity—The Playboy," and still another two-program effort was devoted to award-winning designs for a suburban and a city church.

The National Council of Catholic Men assisted in presentation of similar efforts, including the three-program "Conscience and The Church," and a two-program discussion devoted to various aspects of freedom within the Roman Catholic Church and the relationship of Church to society. Additional Catholic programs dealt with the history of a famous church and the role of the Catholic layman in his church and in society from colonial to modern times.

Perhaps the most moving of the single programs carried by *Look Up and Live* during the survey year was a presentation, offered in cooperation with the New York Board of Rabbis as one of the programs serving the Jewish faith, of the poetry and drawings by some of the 15,000 doomed children of Terezin Concentration Camp in Czechoslavakia during the period from 1942 to 1944. The touching quality of their words, juxtaposed with their paintings and drawings, inspired at least two similar efforts during the year—one a program by NBC-TV (see below) and the other a film by the distinguished Canadian Broadcasting Corporation film-maker, Grahame Woods.

Perhaps the highlight of the *Look Up and Live* season, however, was an hour-long special in which Hector Berlioz's oratorio-trilogy, "L'Enfance Du Christ," was presented in pageant form. Here, as in "The Final Ingredient," and similar NBC-TV work, the full play of network programming resources was in clear evidence.

Lamp Unto My Feet

This series has also evolved a pattern of consultation with various faith groups, but by avoiding any visual identification of the advisory bodies associated with programs *Lamp Unto My Feet* has maintained a flexibility which, according to Producer Pamela Ilott, "allows us greater freedom in dealing with the little, 'non-pressure' groups." Thus *Lamp* has often been able to present programs emphasizing the broader truths which underly all religious faiths. Programs have featured representatives from the Syrian Orthodox or Quaker sects and discussions of the nature of the Hindu and Buddhist religions.

In the survey year *Lamp Unto My Feet* offerings included theological discussions, programs dealing with the arts, special "tri-faith" programs emphasizing the ecumenical movement, and other dramatic, documentary and discussion programs ranging over broad interests and concerns. Among the highlights of the season were a presentation of music for the Jewish High Holy Days which featured Aline McMahon as narrator and the singing of Jan Peerce. "Ceremony of Innocence," a suite of dances by the John Butler Dance Theater based on six poems of Gerard Manly Hopkins, was among the many critically-acclaimed offerings of the year.

The stimulating and imaginative work of the CBS-TV unit earned plaudits in the form of two major awards during the survey year. The New York Board of Rabbis gave an individual award to Miss Ilott for her "Contribution to Religious Broadcasting," and the Catholic Inter-American Co-operation Program presented an award to CBS-TV for the *Look Up and Live* program, "Not By Faith Alone."

NBC Television Network

Of the 52 weekly programs carried in the NBC-TV religious schedule during the survey year, 24 were presented on the *Frontiers of Faith* series, produced in cooperation with the National Council of Churches. *The Catholic Hour,* in cooperation with the National Council of Catholic Men, was seen 16 times. *The Eternal Light* was offered eight times. Two programs were presented as "The Southern Baptist Hour." "I Believe" was a single program, presented in cooperation with the Lutheran Church— Missouri Synod and "Faith and The Bible" was a single offering presented with the cooperation of the American Council of Christian Churches. In addition to these, the Religious Program Department of NBC produced several programs which were offered outside the regular weekly time period.

Frontiers of Faith

During the survey year Dr. Hagen Staack, a scientist-turned-minister whose lectures on the bible are characterized by wit and good humor, delivered a series of lectures entitled "Prophetic Voices of the Bible." (Dr. Staack was given a Gabriel Award for his work in the preceding season.) Dr. Browne Barr of the Pacific School of Religion offered a series of lectures on the parables of Jesus and their present day application, and Dr. Leonidas Contos of the University of Southern California's Graduate School of Religion delivered a series of lectures entitled "The City of God and The City of Man."

The Catholic Hour

Among the 16 programs carried in *The Catholic Hour* during the survey year was included a four-part series on mental illness, "Images of Hope," for which William F. Lynch, S.J., prepared the scripts. Dramatic and documentary techniques were combined in the programs, with dramatic vignettes alternating with actuality film clips, photographs, prints and paintings. "The Images of Hope" series was honored by the American Foundation of Religion and Psychiatry, which extended to NBC-TV one of its first annual media awards for "contribution to greater understanding of work in the field of Religion and Psychiatry." In the same year *The Catholic Hour* featured a four-program study of the Roman Catholic Church in Holland and West Germany— "The Church and Change." These programs were among several taped in Europe by the NBC unit during the season. Through interviews with many members of the hierarchy, theologians and lay experts, the four reports explored current developments and problems of the church in those two countries. *The Catholic Hour* (in 1969 NCORT renamed it *Guideline*) also featured a dramatization of Leo Tolstoy's short-story masterpiece, *The Death of Ivan Ilych,* and "The Prophet," Robert Crean's prize-winning drama about a college student who meets his death in a racial crisis. Four such dramas were staged on *The Catholic Hour* during the survey year, including an original comedy-drama (also by Robert Crean), "The Novice," which related the story of a bishop who feels himself caught in the middle of the conservative-liberal dialogue present in the modern Catholic Church.

The Eternal Light

The venerable series, which playwright Irve Tunick once described as a "gentle Gibraltar of the ether," presented several programs of varying design and purpose throughout the survey year. Among discussion and interview programs presented were a two-part series of colloquies—taped at Oxford and Cambridge Universities—which joined a Protestant and a Catholic clergyman together with a Rabbi for a discussion of ethics in our time. Another program, devoted to the career of the late Senator Herbert Lehman, featured a commentary by Vice-President Hubert H. Humphrey. In still another discussion program, Pauline Frederick of NBC News interviewed Dr. Isador I. Rabi, Nobel Prize winning Professor of Physics at Columbia University, concerning what he considered the artificial separation between the sciences and humanities in our culture, and in yet another program of the discussion type, Mark Van Doren and Maurice Samuel reviewed dramatic moments in the Bible.

Among dramatic programs presented on *The Eternal Light* in the period surveyed were "The Thief and The Hangman," a fable about moral man in an immoral society, and "Days of Awe," presented as a special program in observance of the Jewish High Holy Days. A special *Eternal Light* colorcast also was based upon the drawings and poems created by the children of the Terezin concentration camp, but was cast in a different production form than the CBS-TV program which used the same material. In *The Eternal Light* production, the drawings and poems were integrated into a dramatic story built around the life of one of the children who survived the horrors of the camp and is now living with her husband and daughter in Prague.

Programs By Other Groups

The regular NBC religious series in the survey year also included one program, "Faith and The Bible," presented in cooperation with the American Council of Christian Churches, and two regular-series programs offered in conjunction with the Southern Baptist Convention. The first of these was devoted to a discussion of Southern Baptist life and growth and the second to the story of John Leland, a little-known figure in American history, whose dedication to freedom led to the creation of the Bill of Rights.

Perhaps the high point of the NBC-TV year in religious programming was a special full-hour color documentary film produced in cooperation with the Southern Baptist Convention—"The Inheritance." This program was a major recreation of biblical history, filmed at ancient sites in Iran, Iraq, Egypt, Jordan and Israel. Narrated by Alexander Scourby, "The Inheritance" surveyed the remains of great civilizations of antiquity in the Middle East. Through surviving writings and physical monuments, many of them unearthed by archeologists only in recent years, the program showed how man moved forward to a belief in one God and to the development of an ethical life within the Judeo-Christian tradition. Perhaps no single religious program of the year earned more acclaim and awards. Veteran NBC cameraman Joseph Vadala was awarded a National Press Photographer's Award for his work on this program and "The Inheritance" earned for NBC the Educational Communication Association *G. Herald Duling Memorial Award in Bible Communication* and the Catholic Broadcasters Association *Gabriel Award.*

As is the case with the description of syndicated programming above, such an overview must become little more than a listing. The purpose, in each instance, however, has been merely to suggest both the quantity and quality of religious programs made available to American audiences in a selected period. In processing this great amount of material the editor is certain that errors, both of commission and ommission, have been made, and for those he alone is responsible.

From the foregoing, the following general observations may be drawn. First, it is patently clear that a tremendous range of intellectual and cultural material of religious design is being transmitted to the home community in America by the local television station. It is also clear that the breadth and depth of expertise,

talent and organization which is applied in network and nationally-syndicated programming can seldom be duplicated at the
local level. Finally, national programming clearly is initiating a
wide variety of explorations into secular life and the social dilemmas of our time, as well as providing religious instruction and
edification, insights into religious history and the significance of
the relationship between culture and religion.

III

LOCAL PROGRAM
DESCRIPTIONS

Notes on Grouping

It came as no surprise to discover that the greatest share of all telecasts included in the survey reflect certain basic patterns of communicative purpose already established within churches themselves. However varied the titles and specific "contents" of programs described below may seem at first glance, it is apparent that only two kinds of function are being performed.

First and foremost, there is that kind of program which attempts to employ the natural capacities of the medium in order to engage the wider community in religious matters. The relevances which are sought in those programs are social, institutional or a combination of both. The basic purposes of communication are to inform, instruct and educate. Under this rubric therefore naturally fall the news, lecture-and-talk, interview, question-and-answer, discussion, educational, documentary, variety and dramatic programs—all of which share not only common presentational techniques, but fundamental similarity in purpose. Here are included the efforts to engage both the adult and youthful audience in reflection upon how religious faith and conviction can or should be related to matters of daily life. Here is where the religious and social natures of man are brought into harmony. Here is where churches review their institutional character. Here is where the lessons of "applied faith" are concentrated—in such varied matters as family problems reports of missionary activities, church history, the expressions of religious concern in contemporary culture, the meaning of institutionalized religious customs, philosophies and practices (and instruction in new departures) and the simple, enduring problems of providing a spiritual undergirding for man as he moves to answer his social commitments. (The reasons for establishing a sub-section on programs for young people are largely technical. Those programs designed especially for education and orientation of youth involve special problems in planning and execution, and these are therefore isolated for the convenience of the reader.)

The second group—including by far the greatest number of TV religious programs in this survey—are those designed to provide some form of worship or inspirational experience. The relevance sought in this broad group is primarily theological. The concentration in content moves away, although not entirely, from a socio-spiritual emphasis to more direct and formalized presentation of the religious experience. (Again, a sub-classification of Seasonal, Holiday and Memorial programs is provided for the convenience of those who will use this volume.)

Within the great number of programs in this group are several discernible sub-classes. One notes, first, a worship program which must be described as unique to the medium—the "television service"—which represents an adaptation of church-service to television. This approach involves the major elements of a formal church service, but is in one way or another abridged or condensed—in almost all cases to the half-hour TV time period. Over 30 of these abridged services were reported, all involving music, a formal sermon and varying other elements—depending upon the denomination sponsoring the service.

Another category of TV services is composed of full church services which are conducted in the studio proper. All elements which would be included in the usual church service are also presented here. Some 30 of these programs were reported, most of which were prepared for viewers of Catholic faith. (The phrase "Mass for shut-ins" is frequently employed in the survey descriptions provided, suggesting the importance which the Catholic church assigns to this aspect of media employment.)

Still a third approach is the full "remote" service carried directly from the church. Perhaps the only true content distinction between remote services from the church and those conducted in the studio lies in such extraneous aspects as the weekly collection and the sound of a congregation singing.

Finally, the greatest number of religious offerings in the survey fall within the general designation of inspiration and meditation. These vary in length, but the general content is normally the sermon or "sermonette" and some musical element.

PROGRAMS OF

RELIGIOUS INFORMATION,

ORIENTATION

AND EDUCATION

OUR BELIEVING WORLD
Boston, Massachusetts

That part of religious prejudice which is caused by ignorance and misunderstanding is combated by this series of programs, which intends to bring to its audience a greater knowledge of the services, symbols, and beliefs of other religions.

Our Believing World, which began in 1951, is a non-sectarian series of varying formats, including dramas, discussions of topics of community importance, community religious events and religious services. It is produced by the station in cooperation with the Massachusetts Council of Churches, the Archdiocesan Radio and Television Director, the Rabbinical Council and other religious groups.

Recent programs of note have included a rabbi's discussion of the need for religious education among today's youth which

stressed the importance of religious education in the lives of children of all faiths, a performance of sacred music by a 43-voice
boys choir and a philosophical and theological discussion with
Dr. Martin Luther King of the Southern Christian Leadership
Conference. A documentary drama indicting anti-Semitic acts by
the Soviet Union featured Edward G. Robinson as the prosecutor
and Arthur Goldberg, Senator Javits, Jan Peerce and others as
witnesses for the prosecution.

NIGHT CALL
Champaign, Illinois

The Champaign County Family Service Director said, *"Night
Call* is the only counseling source used by a large number of people in the area." It is this basic need of counseling which accounts
for the popularity of this program. Furthermore, through the
easily accessible medium of television it can provide counseling in
a wide variety of matters for people who often are frightened of
face-to-face meetings with religious or professional counselors.

Two unique features of *Night Call* contribute to its favorable
reception. First, it is a late night show and its setting creates an
atmosphere that matches the informality of the viewer's home.
Because he can telephone in questions, the viewer considers himself a vital part of the program. The second unique feature of
Night Call is that the program is live and "open end"—often
running to 1:30 or 2:00 A.M. This gives the viewer a sense of
control over the conversation. Faithful viewers make regular use
of a reading list of valuable books and pamphlets which relate to
Night Call subjects. The list is kept up-to-date and offered to
the audience without charge.

Programs are designed to present the viewer with information
in those areas where counseling is frequently sought. Among
topics covered are "Youth—Their Manners and Morals," "Conversation with a Gynecologist," "Emotional Instability," "Catholics and Protestants Face Their Differences," "Preparing for Mar-

riage," "Pre-Marital Intercourse and Interpersonal Relationships" and "Labor and Management."

In departures from the normal phone-in format, *Night Call* often presents such special programs as "A Marriage Quiz." For this program viewers could obtain a copy of the answer sheet beforehand, and two sample groups took the test in advance to check scores. Two weeks after the initial "Marriage Quiz," a second program was devoted to questions from viewers who sent in their answer sheets. Many disagreed with the answers provided or simply wished to tell about their own experiences.

DIALOGUE
Detroit, Michigan

Better understanding of the similarities and differences of the world's major theologies is the purpose of *Dialogue,* a weekly 30-minute series broadcast on Sunday mornings. By comparing their faiths, the clergymen seek to give viewers of all religious persuasions a clearer insight into their theologies. The open, discursive quality of the show makes it well-suited to present frank appraisals of both secular and sacred themes.

Each program features a discussion by two and sometimes three representatives of major faiths. The series began in 1964 and elicited more mail and telephone response than any previous religious program on the station. It has been honored with a National Certificate of Merit from the Catholic Broadcasters Association of America.

Topics discussed on the program have included: the role of priest and minister in church and society, responsible parenthood, life after death, the meaning of prayer and education as a state-church issue.

Two cameras are used to videotape the program which requires one hour rehearsal by the participants and two hours of preparation by station personnel.

PLANNING FOR TOMORROW
Fort Worth, Texas

Employing a panel-discussion format, *Planning For Tomorrow* is directed at teachers who are preparing Sunday School lessons. Each week, four representatives of major denominations participate in this 30-minute color program and it attracts not only teachers, but people who are planning to attend Sunday School classes and those generally interested in learning more about the Bible.

The program, which was initiated in 1961, is taped in advance for playback at 7:00 A.M. Saturdays. It is unrehearsed; participants receive only a general outline of the discussion topic upon their arrival at the studio. Past discussions have investigated how problems can be solved through religion, the meaning of Lent, the dangers of hypocrisy and self-righteousness, and the meaning of spiritual blindness. Representatives of several denominations take part.

Two cameras are used for the production, with four hours of preparation by the participants. The station reports good community response.

TELE-COLLEGE
Greenville, South Carolina

Inaugurated in 1964, this program makes available to the public a three-credit college course in religion. The program is produced in full color on a Monday-Wednesday-Friday schedule. The chairman of the religion department at Furman University conducts the course in a studio-classroom with participating students.

The first semester's topic was "The Life and Teachings of Jesus" and it was geared to the freshman level. The program was so successful that more challenging courses were later offered. Among other course-titles available for graduate or undergraduate credit were "The Life and Letters of Paul," "Jesus and His Teachings" and "Christian Doctrine."

The South Carolina Educational Television Center requested and received tapes of the program, which represented the first course offered for college credit over that area's ETV network. The program, however, appeals to non-students as well—as indicated by an encouraging level of audience response.

BIBLE SURVEY
Jackson, Mississippi

Many programs which deal with the Bible are informal in nature, and frequently are intended for a young audience. *Bible Survey* is an exception: it offers formal training in Bible study, intended for adults. Appropriately, the setting for the program is that of a classroom rather than a church or chapel and religious exercises such as prayer or hymns are not used.

The format is very simple. The instructor outlines the purpose of the program, which is to present an over-all survey of the Bible, and then reads the section of the Bible to be covered that day, adding his comments. The instructor, a professor of theology at the Reformed Theological Seminary in Jackson, has been teaching the Bible at the college and seminary level since 1954, and is thus able to lecture without reference to notes or script. He does use a blackboard and Bible maps to illustrate his discussions.

Although the course is being taught by a Presbyterian, a studied attempt has been made to keep the instruction from becoming sectarian. The instructor tries to state fairly the varying views held by theologians on matters open to differences of opinion, without showing his own bias.

Bible Survey is offered by the Reformed Theological Seminary as a college credit course, carrying three credits each quarter. A tuition charge of $15 per quarter is charged those who wish to take the course for credit. The requirements for receiving credit include writing a term paper on the material covered and passing an examination given at the end of the quarter. Because the demands of the course are heavy, the number of people taking the course for credit has been small. Many people also feel that they get full benefit from the course by simply auditing it, without taking the steps necessary to receive credit.

Although the program was originally presented five days a week, the study of the remaining New Testament epistles is now being presented on a once-a-week basis.

THE PASTORS' STUDY
Jefferson City, Missouri

Long before the great upsurge in telephone talk programs, *The Pastors' Study* was taking calls on the air from viewers with questions about religion and their personal problems. The 30-minute, live program, presented weekly since 1955, is broadcast Wednesdays in prime time.

Originally the program was hosted by an Episcopal minister. In 1964, however, the format was changed to include two clergymen, presently a Catholic priest and a Baptist minister, in order to provide greater diversity in the answers given to viewers' questions.

The station broadcasts this sustaining program in prime time because it feels it is able to do more good for more people in this time period than in a less desirable one. Station officials are pleased that the audience response to the program is good despite the fact that it competes with prime-time entertainment programming.

PLAIN TALK WITH PASTOR JERRY
Omaha, Nebraska

This weekly, 30-minute color series provides not only a discussion by the host, but interviews, church news, panel dicussions and music. *Plain Talk With Pastor Jerry* has been telecast on Sunday mornings since 1961, and is primarily aimed at shut-ins and the unchurched. The host, who operates Omaha's Open Door Mission for alcoholics (and is himself a former alcoholic), freely describes his past experiences at the Mission. The program is designed to be informal, instructive and inspirational at the same time rather than "churchy."

Special features include a young people's panel made up of area college students who discuss the relationship of Christianity to today's youngsters, a performer who uses magic tricks to convey an inspirational message to the audience, and a counseling session on current problems faced by families. Community involvement is developed through these special features and through the dedication of a musical number to a rest home or care center in the viewing area, which is notified in advance.

During holiday seasons, a regular guest on the program is the director of the Omaha Safety Council who urges safety on the highways and discusses the subject with the host. During the "Plain Talk" segment, the host discusses Christianity and its relation to today's world. The setting for this portion of the program changes from week to week, while the church news and interviews are conducted from a permanent "pastor's study" set.

Another permanent fixture is a large old pulpit Bible which is used during the closing moments of the program. The host reads a portion of the Scriptures related to the subject of his talk and then recites a short prayer.

THE MASS IN ENGLISH
Omaha, Nebraska

Television can be used not only to present established ideas, but also to inform its audience of changes in recognized institutions. Its function as a familiarizing agent is invaluable in the area of religion, where, too often, complex ideas are treated as "mysteries."

Three days after Roman Catholic churches began celebrating the Mass in English, this hour-long, one-time-only program presented an explanation of the historic change. Monsignor Edward McCaslin of the Omaha Archdiocese celebrated parts of the Mass in English in a special studio setting. An explanation of the event was presented by a clergyman while a 20-voice choir participated. A special message from the Archbishop was also read.

Three cameras were used on the program with one hour rehearsal; two hours preparation by studio personnel; 16 hours by participants.

NEW DIRECTIONS
Philadelphia, Pennsylvania

From its beginning, this program has tried to explore the participation of Catholics in many fields and their contributions to a changing world. To accomplish this goal, *New Directions* has reviewed the Catholic's role in education, art, communications, business and Ecumenism. The validity of the program's discussions derives from the panels composed of well informed Catholic clergy and laity who are active in these diverse fields.

The initial program looked at Catholic education from the viewpoints of a group of teen-agers who are students of local Catholic schools. Their many candid opinions led naturally to subsequent discussions in which nuns considered the changing aspects of their role. The following eight programs highlighted the nuns' views of Liturgical Art, their evaluation of today's theater and examples of their work with disadvantaged and crippled children.

New Directions enlarged its scope for the next eighteen programs by including in-depth discussions of Ecumenism by Catholic clergy and representatives of the Protestant and Jewish faiths. Additional panels focused on such topics as "The Vatican Council and the Jews," "The Liberty of Conscience," "War and Peace," "Vatican II and Communications" and "Vatican II—the Future." One special, hour-long program on the events of Vatican II brought together panelists who were observers at the Council.

A continuing concern with Ecumenism was reflected in the last program of the season, titled "The Ritual of Baptism." Four participants explained the universality of Baptism through the effective use of instruction and modern liturgical symbols.

The entire series enjoyed such wide acceptance that it was scheduled for rebroadcast during the summer.

WHAT'S RIGHT TODAY?
Portland, Oregon

This series is designed to relate the Bible to ethical and moral questions of our time. Each program begins with a brief dramatic skit in which a basic moral question is posed but not answered.

The discussion which follows the dramatic scene attempts to build a Biblical and ethical foundation relating to the theme of the week. The aim of this dicussion is not simply to raise questions, but to provide what the host feels are the Christian answers. The questions raised and the positions taken by the minister-host are intended to stimulate further questions and reactions in church-school classes. A study guide, sent free on request from the Council of Churches, provides a list of topics, Biblical references and pertinent questions. About 1500 have been distributed.

A recent series of thirteen programs dealt with the following topics: euthanasia, sex and promiscuity, birth control and abortion, divorce, politics, business, smoking, drinking and narcotics, gambling, driving, race relations, non-violence and civil disobedience, human welfare and foreign aid and co-existence and war. Questions raised in the latter program included justification of preventive war, bombing the Red Chinese nuclear installations, trading with Communist nations, the theory of deterrence and how peace is to be achieved.

CHURCH OF OUR FATHERS
Raleigh, North Carolina

Evangelism through a mass medium is the fundamental goal of *Church of Our Fathers*. The heart of a typical program is the coverage of the important news stories of all denominations, regardless of their size. This news report incorporates film clips and still pictures, utilizing the techniques of regular news reporting.

The church news is followed by religious songs. The format calls for a different choir, soloist or musical group every week. Choirs provide their own accompanists and may use either a piano or organ or both. Musicians are made aware that this is not a "performance," but a witness to their Christian faith. A minister or lay teacher is featured in the next segment of the program. He highlights the next week's International Lesson, and also delivers Scripture readings, lesson truths and a closing prayer.

The ending of the program features varying elements—interviews, a special travelogue, or a panel discussion. Missionary, church, lay and civic leaders appear during this segment to discuss community projects in which the church may engage—highway safety, conservation of natural resources or recreational and educational opportunities. Often the interview or panel members are national figures.

INSIGHT
San Francisco, California

There are a number of ways to communicate theological and ethical ideas to an audience. Perhaps the most effective means is drama. *Insight,* a weekly anthology, uses the dramatic form to explore in a compelling way the great spiritual conflicts of contemporary society.

Recent programs have dealt with such powerful themes as mental retardation, the collision of love and hate at Auschwitz, teen-age rebellion, a secretary, her boy friend and morality, social justice in Latin America and racial prejudice in America.

Father Ellwood Kieser, C.S.P., the series' creator and host, is an ordained Paulist priest, six feet, six inches tall and looks more like a professional basketball center than a man dedicated to introducing God to the television audience. He has been able to persuade some of the entertainment industry's most successful and talented writers and actors, some Catholic, some not, to join with him in making the episodes of *Insight.* Their services, like his, are donated. Recent programs have featured such stars as Jane Wyman, Efrem Zimbalist, Richard Egan, Vera Miles, Pat Crowley, Henry Silva, Jack Klugman, Brian Keith and Edmund O'Brien. *Insight* is distributed to over 200 stations.

CHALLENGE
Seattle, Washington

This pioneering discussion show has been on the air for seven years and the station plans to continue it "as long as the panelists are willing." The program brings together a Methodist minister, a Roman Catholic priest and a rabbi, who discuss important problems of common interest.

The program was conceived just prior to the 1960 Presidential campaign. The prospective election of a Roman Catholic president had caused emotion to blur understanding of the religious implications. *Challenge* was created to allay fear and combat prejudice by discussing the issues from a clear and dispassionate interfaith standpoint. The program's continuing intent, according to a participant, is "to present the views of the three major faiths with unchallenging respect, thus appealing to viewers to form their own conclusions in the light of the discussion." The "challenge," therefore, is to the viewer.

One of the ground rules for *Challenge* is that it be unstructured, spontaneous and unrehearsed. The panel members do "homework" on the general topics, but specific questions are not discussed until the actual taping. Because many of the topics have been quite controversial, shows are often highly relevant to the everyday lives and decisions of viewers. Subjects of discussion have included: the Supreme Court decision on prayer, birth control, the right to dissent, censorship of movies and conscience in the arts. Program topics are suggested by viewers, community leaders and by the panelists themselves.

Challenge has consistently received strong local support and has been the recipient of several national awards, including the Brotherhood Award from the National Conference of Christians and Jews. This recognition reflects the success of *Challenge* as a program which provides an opportunity to "listen with respect to the opinions of others."

Programs of Religious News

Bay City, Michigan
SCOPE   A weekly news compendium, compiled by the staff of the *Catholic Weekly*, reported by a local priest. Produced in cooperation with the Catholic Charities of Saginaw Diocese. Friday evening; 15 minutes.

Buffalo, New York
RELIGION TODAY   The religious editor of a Buffalo-area-newspaper writes and delivers a religious newscast, delivered at sign-on

and sign-off. Monday, Wednesday, Friday and Sunday; five minutes.

Champaign, Illinois
EVENSONG   In a segment of the Sunday evening news, a clergyman selected by the Religious Radio-Television Committee of East Central Illinois talks about a social or moral problem which frequently relates to an event in the news. The clergymen prepare their own material. Sunday night; five minutes.

Columbia, South Carolina
1 O'CLOCK REPORT   At the close of the regular daily half-hour news report, a clergyman presents five minutes of comments relating religion to the day's events. Monday-Friday afternoon; five minutes.

Columbus, Ohio
SUNDAY MORNING REPORT   This program reports national, international and local religious news. A five-minute commentary by a local clergyman is also given. Sunday morning; half-hour.

Columbus, Ohio
CHURCH BULLETIN BOARD   This program presents announcements and news sent in by local churches. Representatives of religious groups also appear. Sunday morning; five minutes.

Dallas, Texas
THE CATHOLIC REPORT   News of the Catholic church and interviews with local clergymen are presented on this weekly program. Produced by the station in cooperation with the Dallas-Fort Worth Diocese. Sunday morning; 15 minutes.

Durham, North Carolina
NEWS OF THE CHURCH   This weekly religious news program presents national, international and local news. It is syndicated on a state-wide basis and produced by the station and the North Carolina Council of Churches. Sunday morning; 15 minutes.

Indianapolis, Indiana
RELIGION IN THE NEWS   These programs consist of about ten minutes of religious news, followed by a five-minute interview with a local personality. Produced with the Church Federation of Indianapolis. Sunday morning; 15 minutes.

Minneapolis, Minnesota
RELIGIOUS NEWS   Religious news of the major faiths is reported in this weekly program. Produced by the station in cooperation with the Minnesota-Dakota Region of the National Conference of Christians and Jews. Sunday morning; 15 minutes.

Oakland-San Francisco, California
RELIGION TODAY   This report of religious news and significant community programs and events features interviews with outstanding religious leaders. Religious organizations provide the participants. Weekday mornings; ten minutes.

Oklahoma City—Tulsa, Oklahoma
RELIGION IN THE NEWS   The program features reports of current happenings and detailed discussions of major events. Wednesday night.

Omaha, Nebraska
RELIGION IN THE NEWS   The Director of Radio and Television for the Nebraska Council of Churches gives a five-minute weekly broadcast of religious news immediately following the regular 6 P.M. newscast. Jointly produced. Saturday evening; five minutes.

Providence, Rhode Island
FACE THE NEWS   The program features discussions by clergymen and laymen of events in the news of the week. Produced jointly by the station and the Rhode Island State Council of Churches. Sunday morning; 30 minutes.

Sacramento, California
RELIGION IN THE NEWS   The program provides a summary of
local religious activity of all churches and church groups in the
viewing area. Noteworthy national and international religious
events are reported and there are interviews and films of local
religious happenings. Sunday morning; 15 minutes.

St. Louis, Missouri
RELIGIOUS REPORTER   Religious news of all faiths is presented.
Produced by the station in cooperation with the National Con-
ference of Christians and Jews. Sunday morning; 15 minutes.

Santa Maria, California
RELIGION IN THE NEWS   A local minister reports religious events
of interest to the community, as well as world events. This ecumenical program is produced jointly by the station and the
Ministerial Association. Saturday evening; 15 minutes.

Savannah, Georgia
RELIGIOUS NEWS OF THE WEEK   A local minister writes and reports local and regional news of religion. Friday morning; ten
minutes.

Schenectady, New York
HEADLINES IN RELIGION   A minister conducts this program in
which important events of the Protestant, Catholic and Jewish
faiths are reported. Produced by the station in cooperation with
the Council of Churches of Albany, Schenectady and Troy. Sunday morning; 15 minutes.

Seattle, Washington
FROM THE DEAN'S DESK   An Episcopalean clergyman discusses
religious and secular events of current interest. Sunday morning;
15 minutes.

Tucson, Arizona
COMMUNITY CALENDAR   Short announcements are made of various religious activities of local interest, such as holidays and fund raising. These are broadcast during "Woman's Report" and at other times. Produced by the station. Friday and other days, if pertinent; one-four minutes.

Religious Lectures and Talks

Albany, New York
COUNCIL OF CHURCHES   This discussion program utilizes a variety of formats. Written and conducted by a representative of the Council of Churches. Sunday morning; half-hour.

Champaign, Illinois
FRIDAY NOON FEATURE   This program is designed to allow the minister to discuss some of the mail received during the week and to explore particular problems in depth. Friday afternoon; five minutes.

Denver, Colorado
CHALK IT UP   The President of the Denver Area Council moderates a panel of three local ministers, while program participants use chalk and blackboard to illustrate Biblical passages and clarify interpretations. Sunday morning; 30 minutes.

Des Moines, Iowa
THE PASTOR'S STUDY   A pastor and his guest, not necessarily a clergyman, discuss contemporary problems faced by individuals in today's society. Produced with the Des Moines Area Council of Churches. Monday-Friday morning; five minutes.

Grand Junction, Colorado
CHURCH OF CHRIST   A guest clergyman of the Church of Christ reads and elaborates on selected passages of the Bible. Friday evening; 15 minutes.

Greenville, South Carolina
THE PASTOR'S STUDY   Informal chats concerning the application of Christian principles to everyday life. Tuesday and Friday morning; five minutes.

Jackson, Mississippi
THE BIBLE SPEAKS   A local pastor discusses important passages in the Bible, illustrating the talks with visual aids. Sunday afternoon; half-hour.

New Britain, Connecticut
JEWISH LIFE   A rabbi and occasional guests hold discussions on current topics of interest to the Jewish community. Sunday morning; 15–30 minutes.

Providence, Rhode Island
BOOK OF BOOKS   A host rabbi discusses important passages from the Bible or plays religious music. Sunday morning.

Salt Lake City, Utah
FROM THE CATHEDRAL   This program presents the ideas, customs and the laws of the Catholic Church, illustrated through discussion and slides. Sunday morning; 15 minutes.

San Antonio, Texas
SECULAR CITY   Catholic teachings and solutions are presented concerning the problems of urban life. Tuesday evening; 30 minutes.

San Francisco, California
THE WORLD OF RELIGION   Protestant, Catholic and Jewish religious organizations rotate in presenting weekly discussions designed to promote interfaith understanding. The Northern California-Nevada Council of Churches cooperates in planning. Sunday morning; 30 minutes.

Spokane, Washington
LIVING   Each program presents a discussion of a particular chapter of the Bible and relates it to contemporary living. Produced by the station in cooperation with local churches. Monday-Friday morning; 15 minutes.

Tyler, Texas
DR. KERR   Through the use of visual aids such as charts and blackboard, Dr. Kerr presents practical solutions to everyday problems of both religious and nonreligious natures. Sunday morning; 30 minutes.

Interview Programs

Beaumont, Texas
DIMENSIONS IN RELIGION   A host directs questions to three clergymen who make up a guest panel which changes each week. The program seeks to be an open forum, while giving the minister or rabbi a platform from which he may present his views. Sunday afternoon; 30 minutes.

Binghamton, New York
CHURCH DAY BY DAY   Clergymen are interviewed by the Executive Secretary of the Broome County Council of Churches. Sunday morning; 15 minutes.

Clearfield (University Park), Pennsylvania
RELIGIOUS AFFAIRS   Nationally-known theologians who visit the campus of Pennsylvania State University are interviewed by students and faculty. Thursday evening, one hour.

Fort Wayne, Indiana
NEWS CONFERENCE '66   This series presents round-table discussions on important events and interviews with prominent religious figures by a panel of newsmen.

Houston, Texas
BISHOP MORKOVSKY   This special program was a talk by the Administrative Coadjutor of the Diocese of Galveston-Houston, who also led a discussion.

Indianapolis, Indiana
CROSS EXAM   Three local newsmen question a guest, usually of some religious prominence. A minister of the Church Federation of Greater Indianapolis acts as moderator. Sunday afternoon and evening; 30 minutes.

New York, New York
INQUIRY   A Paulist Father serves as host in discussions on a variety of topics relating religion to contemporary life. The Roman Catholic Archdiocese of New York advises. Sunday morning; 30 minutes.

Pittsburgh, Pennsylvania
ENCOUNTER   This program discusses individual encounters with religion and religious education. Produced jointly by the station and the Diocesan Association. Sunday morning; 30 minutes.

San Antonio, Texas
CONVERSATION   Two newsmen interview church leaders from various denominations. The clergymen are selected with the advice of the San Antonio Council of Churches. Sunday afternoon, once a month; 30 minutes.

San Francisco, California
DIVISION IN HIS HOUSE   Interviews and on-location discussions are held by members of the California Migrant Ministry, migrant workers, and rural clergymen. Produced by the station in cooperation with the California-Nevada Council of Churches. Tuesday evening; 30 minutes.

Sioux Falls, South Dakota
LOOK UP AND LIVE   A local pastor interviews experts from various walks of life to determine how religion has affected or influenced their success. Sponsored by the First Lutheran Church. Saturday morning; 15 minutes.

Washington, D. C.
JEWISH COMMUNITY HOUR   This program presents interviews, drama, discussion and news of interest to the Jewish community. Sunday morning (third and fifth Sundays of month); 30 minutes.

Washington, D. C.
VERY IMPORTANT PEOPLE   Using interview and discussion techniques the host of this program, which is produced in cooperation with the Council of Churches of Greater Washington, talks with several guests who share similar occupations of community service. Sunday morning; 30 minutes.

Washington, D. C.
SUNDAY SPOT   A husband-and-wife team interviews guests who perform sketches, show works of art, or discuss matters of current interest. Announcements of religious activities are also given. Produced with the Council of Churches of Greater Washington. Sunday morning; 30 minutes.

Question and Answer Programs

Amarillo, Texas
RELIGIOUS QUESTIONS   Viewers submit questions on all aspects of religion to a panel consisting of a rabbi, a Presbyterian minister, a Catholic priest and a rector of an Episcopal church. Produced by the station and the Amarillo Ministerial Association. Sunday morning; 30 minutes.

Baltimore, Maryland
TO PROMOTE GOOD WILL   Each week a group of students meets with a regular panel consisting of Protestant, Catholic and Jewish clergymen to ask questions and discuss the moral challenges of our daily lives. Produced in cooperation with the American Legion. Monday evening; 30 minutes.

Bluefield, West Virginia
ASK THE PASTOR   Two local pastors answer viewers' questions which are either mailed or phoned in. Topics range from Biblical questions to moral and personal problems. Sunday afternoon.

Bristol, Virginia
CATHOLIC QUESTION BOX   Catholic laymen answer questions sent in by the predominantly Protestant audience. Produced by the station in cooperation with St. Ann's Catholic Church. Sunday morning; 15 minutes.

Chicago, Illinois
QUIZ AND QUOTE   This weekly quiz program dealt with the doctrines, personalities and history of the Roman Catholic Church. A priest from the Communications Center of the Archdiocese of Chicago served as religious expert. Sunday morning; 30 minutes.

Chicago, Illinois
METROTALK (METRO-FORUM)   Two experts who represent different points of view respond to questions put to them by members of the studio audience, by people in the street, by other authorities (via long-distance telephone), and by the Protestant minister who acts as moderator. Jointly produced with the Church Federation of Greater Chicago. Sunday afternoon; 30 minutes.

Dallas, Texas
THE EPISCOPAL CHURCH   Two priests of the Episcopal Diocese discuss church doctrine and answer questions received from view-

ers. Produced by the station in co-operation with the Episcopal Diocese. Sunday morning; 15 minutes.

Dothan, Alabama
ASK THE RABBI   A local rabbi answers questions concerning Judaism, which are mailed and phoned in by the viewing audience. First Monday night of the month; 15 minutes.

Fort Worth, Texas
CHRISTIAN QUESTIONS   A panel of three pastors answer mailed-in questions on the Bible, the church and problems of everyday life. Sunday morning; 30 minutes.

Knoxville, Tennessee
PASTORS' STUDY   Questions on the Bible and other religious topics which have been written or phoned in by viewers are discussed by a panel of three or four clergymen representing several different denominations. Saturday afternoon; 30 minutes.

Los Angeles, California
QUIEN LO SABE?   This program features a panel of priests and laymen who answer questions on religious matters sent in by the audience. In Spanish. Produced with the cooperation of the Archdiocese of Los Angeles. Sunday afternoon; 30 minutes.

Los Angeles, California
CONFRONTATION   Two college students question two clergymen under the guidance of a permanent moderator. Before the broadcast the clergymen are told the subject of the questioning but not the specific questions. The Council of Churches, local colleges and over 100 ministers are actively associated with the program. Sunday afternoon; 30 minutes.

Minneapolis-St. Paul, Minnesota
QUIZ-A-CATHOLIC   Viewers are the principal source of questions in this program patterned along the lines of an entertainment panel quiz. Sunday morning; 30 minutes.

Portland, Oregon
PROBLEMS FAMILIES FACE   A minister and his wife discuss the problems of marriage and raising a family, generally in response to questions and comments sent in by viewers. Produced by the station with the TV Commission of the Council of Churches. Sunday morning; 30 minutes.

Rochester, New York
THE PASTORS' STUDY   Viewers call in their religious questions and receive answers from a local minister and a weekly guest clergyman. Produced by the station in cooperation with the Rochester Area Council of Churches. Thursday morning; 30 minutes.

St. Louis, Missouri
QUIZ-A-CATHOLIC   A panel of laymen and clergymen try to identify objects, events, personalities and teachings of the Catholic Church. Produced by the station in cooperation with the Radio and TV Department of the Archdiocese of St. Louis. Sunday morning; 30 minutes.

Topeka, Kansas
YOUR QUESTION PLEASE   A panel of ministers answer questions written or phoned in by viewers. Saturday afternoon; 30 minutes.

Discussion Programs

Albany, New York
THE BIBLE TODAY   This discussion program is sometimes general in nature, sometimes sectarian. Produced in cooperation with the Tri-City Council of Rabbis. Sunday morning; 15 minutes.

Baltimore, Maryland
THE GOOD NEWS   Three or four guests join with a priest to discuss current questions relevant to religion. Although produced by the Radio-Television Department of the Archdiocese of Baltimore

the program is not limited to Catholic questions or guests. Sunday morning; 30 minutes.

Baltimore, Maryland

FAITH TO FAITH   A Protestant minister and Catholic priest engage in a dialogue exploring areas of agreement and conflict in their theologies. The station cooperates with the Council of Churches and Archdiocese of Baltimore. The United Presbyterian Church distributes the series to stations in ten cities. Tuesday evening; 30 minutes.

Boise, Idaho

INSPIRATION FOR LIFE   A Methodist minister discusses timely topics and interviews guests including clergymen and laymen representing many different denominations. Sunday afternoon; 30 minutes.

Boston, Massachusetts

TURNING POINT   Guests discuss the benefit they have derived from their experience with religion. Produced by the station and Tremont Temple. Sunday morning; 15 minutes.

Bowling Green, Ohio

A CONVERSATION WITH. . . . This series comprised six discussions by faculty members of Bowling Green State University and off-campus guests on the relationships between religion and the academic disciplines. The seminars were organized by the United Christian Fellowship at the University. Monday evening; 30 minutes.

Buffalo, New York

SOCIAL CHRISTIANITY   Discussions and dramatizations of current problems and their solutions encountered by people in all walks of life. Produced by the station in cooperation with the Catholic Diocese of Buffalo. Sunday morning; 30 minutes.

Buffalo, New York
CHALLENGE   Discussion of the role of the church today, and how
religious philosophies deal with problems of the age. Produced
through the Erie County Council of Churches. Sunday afternoon; 30 minutes.

Champaign, Illinois
MORALITY AND THE NEWS   A panel of clergymen discuss topics in
the news sometimes based on suggestions phoned in by the viewers. Produced by the station and the Religious Radio-TV Committee of East Central Illinois. Saturday afternoon, alternate
weeks; 30 minutes.

Charleston, South Carolina
SAINTS AND SINNERS   Members of the Charleston Ministerial Association conduct panel discussions on timely religious and personal problems. Sunday morning; 30 minutes.

Chicago, Illinois
PERSONS, PLACES AND THINGS   To provide Chicago's large Roman
Catholic community with authoritative topical discussion by both
Catholics and non-Catholics the Broadcast Department of the
Archdiocese of Chicago cooperates with the station in presenting
this program. Sunday morning; 30 minutes.

Chicago, Illinois
OUTLOOK   Discussions on the theme that Christian principles
provide the way to solve everyday problems and maintain a
healthy mental outlook. Sunday and Monday morning; 15 minutes.

Chicago, Illinois
WONDERFUL WORLD   The problems of the secular world are examined from a religious point of view through discussions with
specialists, films and dramatic presentations. Produced with the

Radio-Television Department of the Church Federation of Greater Chicago. Saturday afternoon; 30 minutes.

Cincinnati, Ohio
THEOLOGY FOR THE LAYMEN Members of the School of Theology for Laymen, which assists in production, and guests are the panelists for discussions of the role of religion in contemporary society. Tuesday evening; 30 minutes.

Cleveland, Ohio
MORAL VIEW A panel of three clergymen representing the major faiths discuss current trends and events from the viewpoint of religious teaching. The program is developed by the station, the Cleveland Area Church Federation, Cleveland Catholic Diocese and the Jewish Community Federation. Sunday morning; 30 minutes.

Cleveland, Ohio
DIALOGUES OF FAITH Guests discuss topics relevant to today's problems on this interfaith program. Jointly produced by the Catholic Diocese of Cleveland, the Jewish Rabbinical Board and the Cleveland Council of Churches. Sunday afternoon; 30 minutes.

Columbus, Mississippi
ANNUNCIATION CHURCH This special series presented five programs of discussion and film on the progress of Annunciation Catholic Church's mission program. Produced by the station in cooperation with the local church. Monday-Friday evening; 30 minutes.

Denver, Colorado
HOUSE OF THE LORD An informal discussion is held by clergymen and lay guests on religious and secular problems in the community. Produced by the station in cooperation with the Denver Area Council of Churches, Rabbinical Council and the Denver Archdiocese. Sunday morning; 30 minutes.

Denver, Colorado
DIALOGUE '65   A priest, rabbi and minister discuss topics of mutual interest to viewers of their respective faiths. Monday evening; 30 minutes.

Denver, Colorado
DENVER ARTISTS AND DENVER CHURCHES   This program presents discussions with artists and architects who have designed churches and fashioned articles for church interiors. The Denver Public Schools co-produce the program with the station. Thursday evening; 30 minutes.

Dothan, Alabama
PASTORS FORUM   Panel discussion produced in association with the Dothan Ministerial Association. Sunday afternoon; 30 minutes.

Evansville, Indiana
THE MORAL VIEW   Informal discussion by a priest, a rabbi and a minister of local and national problems. Sunday noon; 30 minutes.

Evansville, Indiana
ITEM   General topics of interest to the community are presented on this discussion program with about 20 minutes devoted solely to religious subjects. Saturday morning; one hour.

Fairbanks, Alaska
UNITY   Clergymen of the Catholic and Protestant faiths discuss topics of mutual interest concerning Christianity. Monday evening; 30 minutes.

Fairbanks, Alaska
OVER THE COFFEE CUP   Discussion by a minister selected by the Fairbanks Ministerial Association. Thursday afternoon; 30 minutes.

Grand Rapids, Michigan
FIFTEEN WITH FATHER The Radio-TV Director of the Grand Rapids Catholic Diocese discusses matters of interest to Catholics and non-Catholics. Sunday afternoon; 15 minutes.

Greenville, North Carolina
MORNING MEDITATION Guests of both religious and secular backgrounds discuss topics of an inspirational nature. Monday-Friday mornings.

Honolulu, Hawaii
DIALOGUE Community leaders and ministers discuss and analyze contemporary problems facing the average person. Sunday evening; 30 minutes.

Hutchinson, Kansas
GUIDELINES A moderator and panel consisting of representatives from different churches discuss selections from the Bible as they relate to everyday living. Produced by the station with the Wichita Council of Churches. Sunday morning; 30 minutes.

Indianapolis, Indiana
FOCUS ON FAITH Clergymen representing the three major faiths discuss religious attitudes and beliefs. Produced in cooperation with the Church Federation of Indianapolis. Sunday afternoon; 30 minutes.

Indianapolis, Indiana
LIVING CHURCH Panels of representatives from different denominations rotate in presenting their views on social problems. Sunday morning; 15 minutes.

Indianapolis, Indiana
INSIGHT Local clergymen discuss religious and world problems suggested by the Church Federation of Indianapolis and letters

from viewers. Produced by the station in cooperation with the Church Federation. Sunday morning; 30 minutes.

Jacksonville, Florida
SUNDAY SCHOOL FORUM   New thoughts, trends and methods of Sunday School teaching are discussed by a panel of ministers. Saturday morning; 30 minutes.

Jacksonville, Florida
RELIGION IS RELEVANT   Three local ministers discuss religious topics of interest to the community. Sunday morning; 30 minutes.

Las Vegas, Nevada
THINK   A priest, minister and two laymen discuss subjects of interest to viewers of all faiths. The station produces the program with the National Conference of Christians and Jews. Sunday afternoon; 30 minutes.

Lexington, Kentucky
THE CHRISTIAN HOUR   Selected ministers from Lexington Christian churches participate in panel discussion on topics of current interest. Sunday; 30 minutes.

Lincoln-Grand Island, Nebraska
ANOTHER VIEW OF THE NEWS   A moderator and four guests, at least two of them clergymen, hold an informal discussion on a particular topic of national or international interest. Produced in cooperation with the Nebraska Council of Churches. Every fourth Tuesday evening; 30 minutes.

Lubbock, Texas
CUTTING EDGE   Several ministers from churches of the local Ministerial Association discuss topics of a religious nature which are of importance to the community. Sunday morning; 30 minutes.

Memphis, Tennessee
ROUNDTABLE FORUM Clergy and lay guests discuss religious, moral, and governmental subjects. Produced by the station in cooperation with the National Conference of Christians and Jews. Sunday noon; 30 minutes.

Miami, Florida
CHURCH AND THE WORLD TODAY Panel discussions and interviews dealing with the religious interpretation of personal and community problems in the Diocese of Miami. Sunday morning; 30 minutes.

Miami, Florida
STILL SMALL VOICE This program presents discussions dealing with law, culture, and contemporary problems relating to Judaism. Produced by the station and the Greater Miami Rabbinical Association. Sunday morning; 30 minutes.

Miami, Florida
MAN TO MAN Four or five clergymen engage in a weekly discussion. Produced jointly by the station and the Greater Miami Council of Churches, with the cooperation of the Greater Miami Rabbinical Association and the South Florida Catholic Diocese. Tuesday evening; one hour.

Milwaukee, Wisconsin
CAMPUS CONVICTIONS Chaplains and students from the University of Wisconsin-Milwaukee conduct discussions which stress participation in religious life on the campus. Every last Sunday of the month; one hour.

Milwaukee, Wisconsin
PEOPLE OF THE BOOK Current events and problems within Judaism are discussed. Produced by the station in cooperation with the Jewish Broadcasting Council. Sunday morning; 30 minutes.

Mobile, Alabama
KNOW YOUR BIBLE   A discussion leader from Plateau Church of Christ and two to four laymen discuss facts about the Bible, and viewers call in questions about the Bible. Sunday morning; 30 minutes.

Moline, Illinois
DIALOGUE   Representatives of the three major faiths discuss their mutual problems. Jointly produced by the station and the Council of Churches. Sunday morning, repeated Thursday morning; 30 minutes.

Monroe-West Monroe, Louisiana
LIGHT FROM THE BOOK OF LIFE   A moderator and guest pastors discuss great chapters and Books of the Bible. The Ministerial Alliances of Monroe and West Monroe cooperate in production. Saturday afternoon; 30 minutes.

New York, New York
OUR JEWISH HERITAGE   Prominent clergymen and Jewish laymen discuss current topics of interest to the Jewish community and to religious scholars. The New York Board of Rabbis helps in the production of each program. Sunday morning; 30 minutes.

New York, New York
THE WAY TO GO   Questions of social, ethical, and religious significance are discussed by the moderator and a guest clergyman or layman active in religious work. Guests are recommended by the Roman Catholic Archdiocese of New York, The Protestant Council of New York and the New York Board of Rabbis. Sunday morning; 30 minutes.

New York, New York
RELIGION IN THE NEWS   Guests of various faiths compare views on topical religious happenings in the news. Produced in co-

operation with the National Conference of Christians and Jews. Monday morning; 30 minutes.

New York, New York

POINT OF VIEW   Protestant, Catholic and Jewish clergymen and laymen discuss their views on communal problems. Jointly produced by the station and the New York Board of Rabbis, Protestant Council of the City of New York and the Catholic Council of Churches of New York City. Sunday morning; 30 minutes.

Norfolk, Virginia

LIVE AND LEARN   Clergymen from the Roman Catholic, Episcopal, and Baptist churches meet with a special guest in a topical discussion. Sunday morning; 30 minutes.

Oklahoma City, Oklahoma

OPEN MIND   This program offers a forum for discussion of the morals of our time, the ecumenical spirit, the role of the church in the community and similar topics. Sunday afternoon; 30 minutes.

Palm Beach, Florida

THE PEOPLE OF THE BOOK   This program consists of discussions, interviews and sermons. Produced with the Jewish Federation of Palm Beach County. Alternate Sunday mornings; 30 minutes.

Pittsburgh, Pennsylvania

DUOLOGUE   A minister and a priest discuss theological questions. The Confraternity of Christian Doctrine of the Catholic Diocese and the Council of Churches serve as consultants. Sunday morning; 30 minutes.

Ponce, Puerto Rico

DIALOGO   This interfaith discussion, conducted in Spanish, is concerned with the philosophical aspects of religion. Thursday evening; 35 minutes.

Portland, Maine
COMMUNITY IN FOCUS This program features interdenominational discussions and interviews, and other varied religious programming. Sunday morning; 30 minutes.

Portland, Oregon
FAITH'S CHALLENGE TO TEENS A moderator and six high school students discuss teenage problems. Produced by the station in co-operation with the Youth Concerns Commission of the Greater Portland Council of Churches. Sunday morning; 30 minutes.

Portland, Oregon
PERSPECTIVES 3 A rabbi, minister and priest discuss important problems facing the world today. Sunday afternoon; 30 minutes.

Presque Isle, Maine
FOCUS: ON THE OPEN BIBLE A clergyman and three or four laymen discuss the meaning of selected Biblical passages. Produced with the cooperation of the Presque Isle Ministerial Association. Sunday afternoon; 30 minutes.

Providence, Rhode Island
ON THIS DAY Topical discussions and occasional special music programs of interest to the Protestant viewer. Sunday morning.

Providence, Rhode Island
DIALOGUE Four clergymen discuss the problems of contemporary life in the light of varying religious heritages. Jointly produced by the station and the Rhode Island State Council of Churches, the Catholic Diocese of Providence, the Evangelical Ministers' Association of Rhode Island and the Syrian Orthodox Church. Sunday morning; 15 minutes.

Providence, Rhode Island
FOUR FAITHS This program provided the means for various religious groups to express their beliefs. Associated in the production

were the Catholic Diocese of Providence, the Rhode Island Rabbinical Association, the State Council of Churches, Polish National Catholic Church, Olney Street Baptist Church, Church of Jesus Christ of Latter Day Saints and the Greek Orthodox Church. Sunday morning; 15 minutes.

Roanoke, Virginia
THE LIGHT OF LIFE   Interdenominational panels and discussions. Produced with the Roanoke Ministers Conference.

St. Louis, Missouri
SUNDAY MORNING   Two hosts, a layman and a clergyman, present a program of religious news, discussion, and commentary. The Metropolitan Church Federation cooperates with the station in producing the series. Sunday morning; 30 minutes.

San Antonio, Texas
TEMPLE BETH-EL SERVICE AWARDS   Presentation of a community award by the temple to an outstanding clergyman in the spirit of brotherhood. Sunday; one hour.

San Antonio, Texas
NEW CATHOLIC WORSHIP   This program presented a detailed explanation of changes in Roman Catholic worship. Sunday; one hour.

San Antonio, Texas
IDEAS IN FOCUS   A priest, minister and rabbi give the clergyman's viewpoint on timely subjects. Produced by the station in cooperation with the San Antonio Archdiocese Office, National Council of Churches, Episcopal Diocese and Temple Beth-El. Sunday afternoon; 30 minutes.

San Francisco, California
HERITAGE   A panel consisting of a priest, minister and rabbi discuss topics of a moral or ethical nature, primarily dealing with personal problems. Produced through the combined efforts of the

station, the Archdiocese of San Francisco, the California-Nevada Council of Churches and the Board of Rabbis of Northern California. Sunday afternoon; 30 minutes.

San Francisco, California
HERITAGE   Religious and lay guests discuss topics relating to the works and teachings of the Catholic Church within the Archdiocese of San Francisco. Documentary films are occasionally shown. Sunday morning; 30 minutes.

San Francisco, California
SEARCH   The Women's College of Notre Dame present programs in which students discuss their social welfare work in the poverty areas of Northern California, with emphasis on religious instruction and education. Sunday morning; 30 minutes.

San Francisco, California
ENCOUNTER   A panel of clergymen and laymen present their views on various religious topics. Sunday morning; 30 minutes.

Sioux City, Iowa
CONCERN   A panel of clergymen discuss religious questions and answers mail received from the audience. Produced by the station with the cooperation of the Sioux City Ministerial Association. Saturday noon, repeated Wednesday morning; 30 minutes.

Sioux Falls, South Dakota
OPEN DOOR   A Catholic priest, Lutheran pastor and Baptist minister discuss morals, faith and the problems of the day. Monday night; 30 minutes.

Spokane, Washington
WORLD OF FAITH   Local civic leaders discuss basic Christian principles relating to everyday life. Produced in cooperation with the Spokane Council of Churches. Sunday morning; 30 minutes.

Springfield, Massachusetts
CONCERN   Three community leaders, experts in their field, discuss a topic of current interest and concern. Joint production by the station and the Massachusetts Council of Churches. Sunday afternoon; 30 minutes.

Wheeling, West Virginia
INSTEAD OF WALLS   A minister and panel of laymen including public officials and teenagers, discuss religious questions, and topics which are related to religious principles. Produced with the cooperation of the Council of Churches. Sunday afternoon; 30 minutes.

Winston-Salem–Greensboro, North Carolina
PARSONS TO PERSONS   A panel of three ministers and a minister moderator answer questions and discuss topics of a religious nature. Seven local churches participate: Lutheran, Baptist, Presbyterian, First Christian, Home Moravian, Centenary Methodist and Episcopal. Saturday afternoon; 15 minutes.

Yakima, Washington
ECUMENISM—LOCAL PROGRESS   New events and doctrines pertaining to Christianity are discussed on this program which includes a panel consisting of two priests and a minister. Tuesday night.

Educational Programs

Binghamton, New York
INTO FOCUS   This broadcast of a Catholic religious class is concerned with matters of Catholic doctrine, sometimes on a catechism level, sometimes on an adult level. Sunday morning; 15 minutes.

Buffalo, New York
MIND OVER MYTH   Produced under the auspices of the Anti-Defamation League of B'nai B'rith this program is intended to

debunk some of the questionable myths and fallacies held by various religious and racial groups. Sunday afternoon, monthly; 30 minutes.

Carthage-Watertown, New York
THE CHURCH ON TELEVISION Representatives of the Catholic and Protestant faiths alternate in presenting their religious opinions and practices. Each program includes an introductory statement, church history, choir selections, sermon or discussion, and a closing statement or prayer. The Jefferson County Council of Churches, St. Lawrence Council of Churches and the Diocese of Ogdenburg cooperate in the production. Sunday noon; 30 minutes.

Charleston, South Carolina
THE LIVING TRUTH Half-hour religious lessons are presented. Saturday morning.

Chicago, Illinois
ETERNAL QUEST A presentation of a point in the history of Judaism is followed by rabbinical discussion of its significance. Produced by the station and the Chicago Board of Rabbis. Sunday morning; 30 minutes.

Columbus, Ohio
HOUSE DIVIDED Christian and Jewish clergymen provide family counseling through the use of dramatizations of problems in domestic relations. Wednesday; 30 minutes.

Columbus, Ohio
TELE-BIBLE TIME Stories and messages taken from the Bible are depicted by the use of sketches prepared by an art professor who is also a Baptist minister. Produced by the station and Cedarville College. Sunday morning; 15 minutes.

Denver, Colorado
MASS IN ENGLISH   This program consisted of a complete Catholic Mass, in English, and was the first such Mass broadcast in the area. Produced under the guidance of the Denver Archdiocese. October 28, 1964; 30 minutes.

Detroit, Michigan
WITH THIS RING   A Catholic priest discussed approaches to marriage and its problems. Sunday morning; 15 minutes.

Lincoln-Grand Island, Nebraska
REFORMATION RALLY   The rally of the Northern Kansas Conference of the American Lutheran Church held in Kensington, Kansas, was filmed and presented by the station. Sunday morning; one hour.

New York, New York
JEWISH FOURTH "R"   Through a variety of formats Jewish religious schools in the area offer enrichment material to supplement formal religious training. Produced with the cooperation of the New York Board of Rabbis. Sunday morning; 15 minutes.

Oakland-San Francisco, California
THE MASS IN ENGLISH   A presentation of the Catholic Mass in English was followed by a discussion among Roman Catholic clergymen concerning this historic change in Church liturgy. September 27, 1964; one hour.

Orlando, Florida
YOUR LIFE IN THE WORLD TODAY   This program treats the problems confronting people as individuals and as members of society, with emphasis on demonstrating the relation between religious belief, life and its challenges. Produced with the Episcopal Diocese of Florida. Sunday afternoon; 30 minutes.

Philadelphia, Pennsylvania
SUNDAY SEMINAR-THE LIGHT WITHIN   Guests discuss the history of Quakerism, using films, slides and other visual aids. Produced by the station and the Philadelphia Yearly Meeting of the Religious Society of Friends, Haverford College, Pendle Hill and American Friends Service Committee. Sunday morning; 30 minutes.

Philadelphia, Pennsylvania
SUNDAY SEMINAR-THE HEBRAIC IMPACT ON WESTERN CIVILIZATION A moderator and guests discuss aspects of the Jewish influence on the Western world. Produced in cooperation with the Federation of Jewish Agencies. Sunday morning; 30 minutes.

Port Arthur, Texas
LESSONS FROM THE BOOK OF AGES   Sunday School lessons are given on this program which features religious thought and instruction. Sunday morning; 15 minutes.

Portland, Oregon
SOUND OF THE BIBLE   This program features audience participation in reading the Bible and includes films and slides. Produced by the station with the Youth for Christ Organization. Sunday morning; 15 minutes.

Providence, Rhode Island
CATHOLIC CHAPEL   A Catholic priest discusses the meaning and symbolism of various practices in the Catholic ritual. Sunday morning; 30 minutes.

Seattle, Washington
LIVING   A chaplain of Whitworth College, Spokane presents a series of lessons on the life and teachings of Christ. Produced by a Spokane station. Monday-Friday morning; 14 minutes.

Steubenville, Ohio-Wheeling, West Virginia
LIVING JUDAISM   Through the use of dramatizations, discussions and interviews, a rabbi presents the practices, philosophy, customs, ceremonies, history and culture of the Jewish faith. Sunday morning, once monthly; 15 or 30 minutes.

Youngstown, Ohio
THAT WE MAY SEE   A current religious book is reviewed on each program. Produced by the station in cooperation with the Diocesan Radio and Television League. Sunday afternoon; 15 minutes.

Documentaries

Baltimore, Maryland
CARDINAL SHEHAN IN ROME   Film sequences made in Baltimore and Rome recorded the ceremonies of the elevation of Lawrence Shehan to Cardinal. Produced by the station. Shown three times during 1965.

Baltimore, Maryland
PURIM THEN AND NOW   Presentation of the history of the Jewish holiday of Purim and of its relation to contemporary social problems. Produced by the station.

Buffalo, New York
A PERSONAL DIMENSION   The filmed first part of this program shows volunteer workers giving religious information and guidance to others; the second presents groups reciting the Rosary. Alternate Sunday afternoons; 30 minutes.

Chattanooga, Tennessee
UPWARD LOOK   Local ministers present this daily documentary. Text and talent are provided by the Chattanooga Ministerial Association. Monday-Saturday mornings; 15 minutes.

Cincinnati, Ohio
Consecration of a Bishop   Catholic ceremonies consecrating a
bishop and a Solemn High Mass were presented on this program.
Afternoon; two hours.

Columbus, Ohio
The Novitiate; The Church and Its Steeple; The High Holy
Days   This series of film-and-tape documentaries included the
story of how a girl becomes a nun, described the inner workings
of a small town Protestant church, and presented the ceremonies
of the Jewish High Holy Days. Produced by the station. September 5, December 13, and September 13, 1964; 30 minutes.

Columbus, Ohio
Installation of a Bishop   This coverage of the installation
ceremony of a bishop, with narration explaining the rituals, received an Emmy nomination. Produced by the station. March 25,
1965, morning; 30 minutes.

Detroit, Michigan
The Consecration of a Bishop   Presentation of the consecration ceremony of the new Suffragan Bishop of the Episcopal
Church of Michigan. Commentary was given by the Canon of the
Cathedral Church of St. Paul, where the ceremony was held. Sunday afternoon; 30 minutes.

Hartford, Connecticut
25 Years a Bishop   An interview with Archbishop O'Brien,
interspersed with film and stills of his career as a Bishop; 30 minutes.

Houston, Texas
The Consecration of a Bishop   Ceremonies consecrating a
Bishop with explanatory narration by an Episcopal minister. September 21, 1964; two hours.

New Orleans, Louisiana
THE WOMAN CALLED SISTER   This two-part documentary, filmed on location, showed how the nun relates to the modern world. Sunday morning; 30 minutes each part.

New Orleans, Louisiana
WHY A CRUCIFIXION   The story of the Crucifixion and its symbolism through the years. Use was made of scenes of the Crucifixion selected from art treasures. Good Friday afternoon; 30 minutes.

New Orleans, Louisiana
THE CASE FOR FATHER SEELOS   Documentary film explaining the Roman Catholic canonization procedures, with reference to the case of Father Seelos who served in New Orleans. April 17, 1965; 30 minutes.

Oakland-San Francisco, California
ORDINATION TO THE PRIESTHOOD   Coverage of the ceremonies of ordination as a Catholic priest from St. Louis Vertrand's Church of Oakland. March 30, 1963, morning; one hour.

Omaha, Nebraska
ORDINATION OF PRIESTS   This program presented the full ceremony of the ordination of nine men entering the Roman Catholic priesthood. Produced by the station with the cooperation of the Archdiocese of Omaha. Saturday morning; two hours.

Omaha, Nebraska
THE QUALITY OF MERCY   Documentary film revealing how young women are trained for the life of a nun, form postulancy through profession of vows, in the Sisters of Mercy Provincial House of Omaha. November 10, 1963; one hour.

Omaha, Nebraska
THIS WE BELIEVE   A film series which focuses on a different church each week, including discussion of the functions and ac-

tivities of the church by the minister, a history of the church, and choral selections. Alternate Sundays; 30 minutes.

Omaha, Nebraska
BISHOP SHEEHAN'S CONSECRATION   Coverage of the full ceremony consecrating a local Bishop. Produced with the assistance of the Archdiocese of Omaha. March 19, 1964; two and one-half hours.

Pittsburgh, Pennsylvania
THE BISHOP RETURNS   The local Catholic Bishop reported the purpose and accomplishments of the Second Vatican Ecumenical Council from which he had just returned. Sunday afternoon; 15 minutes.

Portland, Oregon
ALTARS OF FAITH   Local churches rotate, presenting such diverse material as studies of religious art and music, sermons, and celebrations of specific holidays. Sunday, late afternoon; 30 minutes.

San Francisco, California
CONSECRATION OF GRACE CATHEDRAL   This program presented the two-hour consecration service at Grace Episcopal Cathedral. Sunday afternoon; two hours.

San Francisco, California
PASSOVER STORY—FROM EXODUS TO SELMA   This program presented a discussion by three rabbis on the meaning of Passover in terms of their participation in the civil rights march from Selma to Montgomery, Alabama. Produced by the station in cooperation with the Board of Rabbis of Northern California. Sunday morning; 30 minutes.

Variety Programs

Albany, New York
CATHOLIC SPOTLIGHT   This program, largely discussion, also includes choir and interview interludes as well as special holiday programs. Jointly produced with the Albany Diocese. Sunday morning; 30 minutes.

Asheville, North Carolina
SEND THE LIGHT   Religious news, reading from the Scriptures, songs, discussion of a feature pamphlet, sermon and prayers. Sunday; 30 minutes.

Charlotte, North Carolina
HOUR OF OPPORTUNITY   Dramatic sketches, music and discussion. Sunday morning; 30 minutes.

Chicago, Illinois
TAKE ONE   Material is drawn from a wide range of the performing, graphic and plastic arts, as well as from the social sciences. Presented by the Communications Center of the Catholic Archdiocese of Chicago. Sunday morning; 30 minutes.

Dallas, Texas
THE BIBLE SAYS   This revival program features a sermonette, discussion, choirs and missionary reports. Produced by the station in cooperation with Radio Revival. Sunday morning; 15 minutes.

Detroit, Michigan
INSIGHT   Drama, discussions, reading and conversation. Jointly produced by the station and the Jewish Welfare Board. Sunday morning; 15 minutes.

Hastings, Nebraska
THIS IS THE CHURCH   Churches, selected on a rotating basis, conduct a half-hour program in a format of their own choosing. Pro-

duced by the Hastings and Grand Island Ministerial Association. Tuesday and Thursday afternoon; 30 minutes.

Houston, Texas
THE PULPIT   Area churches present programs of varied formats prepared by the selected church. Sunday morning; 30 minutes.

Johnstown, Pennsylvania
RELIGION TODAY   Representatives of all faiths present programs which they design. Wednesday afternoon; 15 minutes.

Kalamazoo-Grand Rapids, Michigan
SUNDAY MORNING SERVICE   Local churches rotate in presenting sermons, dramas, discussions, documentaries, dialogues and religious art. Sunday morning; 15 minutes.

Los Angeles, California
SUNDAY STORY TIME   Variety program designed for both an adult and children's audience. Produced by the Southern California Council of Churches with the participation of the Roman Catholic Church and the Jewish Council. Sunday morning; 30 minutes.

Los Angeles, California
LA HORA CATOLICA   Interviews, religious art, discussion and Bible lessons in Spanish. Produced with the Archdiocese of Los Angeles. Sunday afternoon; 30 minutes.

Lynchburg, Virginia
PROJECT RELIGION   Contents varies—discussion, dramatic adaptations of Bible stories and secular problems, choirs and music. Produced by the Lynchburg Ministerial Association. Sunday afternoon; 30 minutes.

Miami, Florida
HORIZONS OF FAITH   A religious variety show intended for Protestant viewers of all ages featuring sermons, songs, children's sto-

ries, book reviews and church news. Produced in cooperation with the Greater Miami Council of Churches and the Fort Lauderdale Ministers Association. Sunday morning; 30 minutes.

Milwaukee, Wisconsin
VIEWPOINT Panel discussions, drama, debates, contests and guest interviews. The Sodality Union of the Milwaukee Archdiocese assists in the production of the program. Sunday morning; 30 minutes.

Milwaukee, Wisconsin
LUTHERAN GUIDEPOSTS Religious panel discussions, dramatic plays, church services, and missionary films. Produced by the station and the Milwaukee Lutheran schools. Sunday morning; 30 minutes.

New York, New York
OUR PROTESTANT HERITAGE A variety of formats is employed to focus on current ideas of religion and morality. Sunday morning; 30 minutes.

Philadelphia, Pennsylvania
SUNDAY SEMINAR—THE PERSUADED Interviews, music and news are featured on this religious variety program moderated by two clergymen. Produced in cooperation with the Greater Philadelphia Council of Churches. Sunday morning; 30 minutes.

Pittsburgh, Pennsylvania
FAITH AND FREEDOM Variety program which attempts to foster knowledge of religion, folklore and the country. Produced by the Jewish Community Relations Council in association with the station. Alternate Sunday mornings; 30 minutes.

Pittsburgh, Pennsylvania
WE BELIEVE An interfaith series for which participants choose the format (documentaries, drama, worship services or discussions) best suited to their message. Assisting the station in produc-

tion are the Catholic Diocese of Pittsburgh, the Eastern Orthodox Clergy, the Jewish Community Relations Center and the Pittsburgh Council of Churches. Four interfaith programs are also presented each year. Sunday morning; 30 minutes.

Portland, Oregon
AND GIVE THEE PEACE   Programs are presented by the Catholic, Jewish and Protestant faiths in a rotating sequence. Each group chooses material it wishes to present. Produced by the station in cooperation with the TV Commission of Greater Portland. Sunday morning; 15 minutes.

St. Louis, Missouri
WAY OF LIFE   Experimental drama, discussion, folk singing and interviews. Produced by a committee of Lutheran pastors and laymen from the Missouri Synod. Sunday morning; 30 minutes.

Springfield, Missouri
IT IS NO SECRET   Interviews, gospel music, religious news, short sermon and invitation. Produced in cooperation with High Street Baptist Church and Baptist Bible College. Saturday afternoon; 30 minutes.

Terre Haute, Indiana
THE GREATEST GIFT   Discussions and other presentation of questions regarding faith and morality in the community. Jointly produced with a number of organizations representing many faiths and denominations. Sunday morning; one hour.

Wheeling, West Virginia
CHRIST IN THE WORLD   Discussion of Bible passages with children, choir music and adult panel discussions. Produced with the Catholic Diocese. Sunday afternoon; 30 minutes.

Dramatic Programs

Binghamton, New York
STORIES RETOLD   This non-sectarian program is produced in co-operation with a local minister who writes and narrates or stages dramatic episodes from the Bible and contemporary writings. Sunday morning; 15 minutes.

Chicago, Illinois
EVERYMAN   Areas of church activity are described, with occasional dramatic segments, by three hosts selected by the Church Federation of Greater Chicago. Sunday; 30 minutes.

Dayton, Ohio
BLESS THIS HOUSE   A ten-minute sketch dramatizing a family problem is followed by 20 minutes of discussion. Produced jointly by the station and the Church Federation of Greater Dayton. Sunday afternoon; 30 minutes.

Philadelphia, Pennsylvania
STORIES RETOLD   Dramatic presentations of Biblical stories. Produced by the station. Sunday morning; 15 minutes.

Washington, D. C.
BREAKTHRU   A group of youngsters discuss a dramatic film segment which deals with family life. Jointly produced with the Washington Council of Churches. Sunday morning; 30 minutes.

RELIGIOUS PROGRAMS

FOR YOUNG PEOPLE

THE MAGIC DOOR
Chicago, Illinois

Produced by the Chicago Board of Rabbis, *The Magic Door* is an anthology of Biblical stories for a predominantly non-Jewish audience. The series became possible in its community after the producer had persuaded the station and other faith groups to alter their rotating schedule of programs. It was felt that an audience could be more effectively built up if there was a continuing, consistent program in the time slot, and it was further reasoned that a children's program would have a larger potential audience at the scheduled Sunday morning hour. The history of *The Magic Door* reveals how religion is adjusting to the demands of specificity in television.

This weekly, videotaped program is aimed at primary-grade children. Each program is designed both to teach and entertain its young audience. The Board of Rabbis supplies guides for the writers of the series, although Ben Aronin, author of children's books, has contributed a great many scripts. Under the name of "Uncle Ben," Aronin also acts as the program's host.

A typical episode opens with a scene in front of "Acorn House." From there, the viewer passes through a magically opened door. After preparation for the idea of a particular program, a "space-time machine" is used to transport the viewer to the era of the story. A great degree of care is devoted to introduction and preparation before the "space-time machine" is used. Each story is told by a narrator and continuing characters, and is illustrated by means of puppets.

Because of the consistently favorable newspaper and mail comment, the Board of Rabbis has made *The Magic Door* available outside the immediate viewing area.

BY GEMINI
Chicago, Illinois

The use of an entertaining situation to communicate more serious ideas has become an increasingly popular element in religious telecasts for children. Presented by the Roman Catholic Archdiocese of Chicago, *By Gemini* presents the adventures of "space priest" Father John, his partner—an eleven-year-old girl named Robin—and their puppet mascot, Booster. The program, which is nonsectarian in nature, is intended for all children eight to twelve years old.

Father John, Robin and Booster seek to stamp out a sinister, anti-religious organization known as STERF (Society for the Total Elimination of Religious Faith). In their battle against STERF, the crew ventures all over the world in a supersonic aircraft. Short films are used to set the mood for the country to be visited. In order to convey messages to his audience without interference from STERF, Father John uses a code—the key to which is sent to viewers upon request.

Presented in color every Sunday morning, *By Gemini* has drawn favorable comment from its audience. One boy wrote: *I think your show is very good. I would like you to write to me. I like when you blast off. I watch you every day. I am nine years old. Please send me the secret code.* A girl asked for the decoder and pictures, diplomatically adding: *I like Robin the best, no affence Father John and Booster.*

KUMZITZ
Chicago, Illinois

The purpose of *Kumzitz,* which is aired each Sunday morning, is to help young people learn more about life by mixing the music they like with serious discussions of matters in which they are interested. Recent topics have included the United Nations, law enforcement (with a captain of the Chicago police department), athletic scholarships (with a Chicago Bears football player), careers in communications (with Irv Kupcinet), violence in the mass media (with the television critic of the Chicago Daily News) and a number of discussions relating Jewish law and custom to contemporary problems.

"Kumzitz" means to come and sit—to gather at someone's home to sit and talk and sing. While young people enjoy the music of the name bands and vocal groups presented on this program, they enjoy even more the opportunity provided to express what they think. The program's philosophy is that it is easy to communicate with young people—if you talk *with* them, not *at* them.

The former executive director of the Broadcasting Commission of the Chicago Board of Rabbis designed *Kumzitz* to be an entertaining learning experience for the young people who take part in the studio and for those at home. He feels that the program "demonstrates that young people like 'rock 'n' roll' and other music, but they still think about what's important. They are greatly concerned about the world around them, their roles in life and how they relate to the generations that have preceded them."

STORIES OF THE KING
Grand Rapids, Michigan

In order to supplement the religious education of children who have little or no access to such training, *Stories of the King* presents a Biblical story each Sunday morning.

The program, produced by a minister and his wife, utilizes a simple format. Visual materials including photographs, original art work, flannel-graphs, flash cards, film strips and other objects, are generously used to attract and hold the interest of youngsters. The minister's wife, who also acts as program hostess, tells the story while using visual aids which relate to it. A studio organist provides appropriate musical accompaniment. The basic approach is to keep the interpretation of the Bible story vivid and alive, and the prime concern is to involve the child in an understanding of Biblical teachings.

The high level of appreciative response has confirmed the minister's conviction that "by using television, we're able to supplement the teaching already received by some children, and to offer Bible teaching to those who are not receiving any through other sources." *Stories of the King* complements the work of the established religious institutions in this area.

TIMOTHY CHURCHMOUSE
Indianapolis, Indiana

In this weekly half-hour series for children the adventures of a puppet character named Timothy Churchmouse and his friends serve as the vehicle for teaching Christian ethics.

Timothy, a hand puppet typifying an eight-year-old child,

lives with his cousin, Kathleen Churchmouse, in a churchtower. Along with other puppet characters (the studious Jeremiah Bookworm, timid little Orvie Mouse, and pompous Mr. Owl), Timothy confronts the challenges of the surrounding world. In order to guide Timothy and his friends with Christian love, maturity and good humor, several "live" characters are woven into the stories. These include Uncle Matthew, an elderly minister who has traveled the world and has a deep insight into all people and a deep love for children; Reverend Good, Miss Peg and old Aunt Agatha.

Through the use of the continuing characters, the program unfolds episodes which stress the basic tenets of Christian concepts and faith and help youngsters to meet the problems of the contemporary world. A wide variety of music, from Brahms to The Beatles, is carefully selected and used both as a background and focal point for miniature animated scenes. The story line is enlivened with special effects such as the magic of "Happy Hands," limbo-fun, live dancers, appropriate slides and pantomime.

Program themes have included concern for others, learning about God, friends in church and religious holidays. Occasionally, an appropriate story or book is used with camera shots of the book illustrations. When a Bible story or quotation will help get a program's theme across, it is woven into the story, often with illustrations and selected music. The program never becomes "preachy."

Timothy Churchmouse, inaugurated in 1957, is a production of the Television Workshop of the Church Federation of Greater Indianapolis. Scripts are donated by both professionals and amateurs during the program's school-year season. Writers, puppeteers, the musical director, and the director each spend about ten hours preparing a broadcast. Mindful that public service programming is compared by the viewer with commercial programming, the production group makes every effort to keep standards consistently high.

MR. BOB SHOW
Kansas City, Missouri

Pre-school children enjoy using their imagination when they make up their own stories. The *Mr. Bob Show* capitalizes upon this tendency in order to help widen the scope of religion for preschool children.

During a typical show, "How Do You Show Love?", Mr. Bob read incomplete stories to a group of children in the studio, who were then asked to supply the endings. These stories, when completed, indicated ways in which they can and do show love to others. As the approach demonstrates, the entire series employs an inductive method designed to give pre-school children an opportunity to discuss and learn about their religion.

Every attempt is made to assure that the content of each program coincides with the seasonal nature of the various denominational curriculae used in the metropolitan churches. This is not particularly difficult since at the pre-school level nearly all denominational curriculum coincides in content and approach. Furthermore, each church expressing an interest in use of the program is offered a syllabus providing them with titles and program descriptions of all programs in one quarter (13 weeks).

The cohesive and appealing character to the children is Mr. Bob, whose image elicits honest and enthusiastic response from his pre-school viewers. He employs a variety of communicative techniques and devices, including hand puppets, marionettes, the Singing Lady and the Story Lady. Bob often uses audio-visual equipment to create special effects, and often utilizes the subjective camera method which represents all the children at home. Through this method the home viewers are asked to respond to his questions and thus become active participants in the program.

BIBLE STORY TIME
Minneapolis-St. Paul, Minnesota

Stories have always provided a fine vehicle for presenting more complicated ideas to children. When the subject is as abstract as religion or "goodness," the use of stories is especially effective.

Through the use of varied formats, *Bible Story Time* presents Biblical stories in a way that makes religion appealing to young children. The program begins with a short object lesson or a personality in order to capture the interest of the audience and to lead into the longer presentation of the Biblical tale. A narrator is always featured, assisted by actors. Together, they utilize such techniques as pictures, puppets, tableaus, dolls, shadow acting, flannel boards and sound effects. Live animals have also been used to illustrate some of the stories. A local minister who is also a skilled cartoonist has presented stories while illustrating his points with cartoons.

Mail indicates that the program fills a void created by lulls in Sunday School programs in many area churches. One mother said of her six-year-old daughter's devotion to the program: "She enjoys it so much, as our church does not have Sunday School during the winter months."

The station provides free air time for the program and broadcasts it in full color. Most of the production work, including art and talent, is contributed by more than 60 volunteers.

THE LITTLE FLOCK
New Bedford, Massachusetts

Although *The Little Flock* is conducted by the Roman Catholic Victory Noll Sisters, it is not intended to be for Catholic children only, but rather offers an opportunity for all children to experience the joy of Christian living.

The program is produced solely by the Sisters who have been trained by the station in the use of the audio and video equipment necessary for the production. Responsibility for planning and preparing each program is, at the Sisters' request, left entirely to them. The video-taped program, which is now seen on Sunday afternoon, is produced by the Sisters in the station's studios. Children from orphanages, religious classes, and parishes throughout the Roman Catholic Diocese of Fall River act as the studio audience.

The program's main feature is a story book borrowed from the library, around which a discussion is planned. Songs, dances, games and projects which relate the story to the child's life are developed. One of the most popular regular features is the appearance of Andy, the hand puppet operated by one of the Sisters. He is a model of good conduct, illustrating the right thing to do. Young viewers seem to identify easily with the good-natured puppet. The stories are not necessarily religious in nature, but are all made to tie in with each program's basic theme.

Besides producing the program, the Victory Noll Sisters also arrange for most of the publicity for the program, from making posters to writing information bulletins. The Sisters also appear before adult groups in order to stimulate their interest in *The Little Flock.*

HOUSE OF HAPPINESS
San Diego, California

When *House of Happiness* first went on the air, the program elements were a religious song by a soloist or duo, and an interview with a person with whom children could associate. When a production team of a minister and his wife was recently appointed (by the San Diego Council of Churches) to conduct the program, a number of new elements were added. It was felt that the program would be improved by having the children directly involved in it, and so each week a group from a different area church takes part. Some groups may re-enact typical Sunday School or Bible study classes. Churches that have youth choirs bring them to the program. These choirs have, in fact, been very popular with both participants and the audience. The lure of appearing on television makes the children in choirs rehearse more faithfully and take a greater interest in this activity because they know their friends and relatives will be watching.

Community involvement has also been sought in other ways. A contest in which children were to draw a picture giving their impression of Easter was conducted for which the station provided a series of weekly prizes, culminating in the presentation of Bibles as grand prizes. Children from all parts of the viewing area submitted drawings which were judged by age groups. The drawings were displayed at a local shopping center during Easter week.

House of Happiness also features the animated film series for children, *Davey and Goliath,* which is supplied by the National Council of Churches and integrated into the format.

RING AROUND THE WORLD
West Hartford, Connecticut

In a departure from traditional religious education, *Ring Around The World* intends to present a contemporary re-statement of some religious ideas which will have meaning for both children and adults. The program's basic premise is the exploration of the wonders of the world. The program setting, the Friendly Forest, provides a natural background for learning about the cycle of the seasons, seeing the plan of God for the preservation and care of animals, and understanding the miracle of growth.

The program intends to stimulate curiosity rather than to give facts, and so encourages its young viewers to discover and explore on their own. In keeping with this philosophy, the program does not include the telling of lengthy stories or extended readings from the Bible. Bible facts and readings from the Bible do often enter into the program, but only if they can be included in a natural way. A program on camping, for example, would include reference to the early nomadic life of the Hebrew people, as well as the reading of selected verses from the Psalms.

By the use of puppetry, music, drama, dance and other forms, the program has stressed the idea that it is good to be alive in a world which is full of interesting things to see and do—a world abounding in exciting discoveries. The program also stresses the building of good relationships with other people.

Ring Around the World intends to deliver its message without sermonizing. It is felt that if what is said, done and suggested on the program is strong enough, no further sermonic comment is necessary. The producers believe that if a concept is well-stated, then there is hope that the viewers will understand at least a portion of the idea. If the concept is not well presented, moralizing will do little to insure a more profound understanding of the idea.

Baltimore, Maryland

QUEST This program presents two teen-agers from each of the three major faiths discussing social and religious issues with a clergyman. The program gives the teen-ager a chance to bare his mind on important issues and to ask questions. Produced by the station with the Archdiocese of Baltimore, Baltimore Jewish Council and the Maryland Council of Churches. Sunday afternoon; 30 minutes; tape; three cameras; studio origination; 45 minutes rehearsal.

Charleston, South Carolina

THE LIVING TRUTH This weekly program features Sunday School lessons for children. Produced by the station. 30 minutes; tape; studio origination.

Cleveland, Ohio

ALL GOD'S CHILDREN Designed to instruct children unable to attend Sunday School, *All God's Children* features a host and five children, who discuss principles of the Christian religion. Pro-

duced by the station in cooperation with the Catholic Diocese of
Cleveland and Kappa Gamma Pi Honorary Society. Sunday
morning; 30 minutes; tape; two cameras; studio origination;
three hours preparation by station; ten hours preparation by participants; 30 minutes rehearsal.

Columbia, South Carolina

A CHILDREN'S CHRISTMAS SERVICE This program, planned for
young viewers, is a shortened and simplified version of the Episcopal Morning Prayer at Christmas. Produced by the station;
morning of Christmas Eve; 20 minutes; tape; three cameras; studio origination; four hours preparation by station; eight hours
preparation by participants; one hour rehearsal.

Columbus, Ohio

WONDERBOX In a kindergarten school setting, six children discuss Bible stories which are read by a Sunday School teacher. Produced by the Council of Churches. Sunday mornings; 30 minutes;
live; studio origination; one camera; two hours preparation by
station; four hours preparation by others; one hour rehearsal.

Greensboro, North Carolina

CHILDREN'S CHAPEL On this program a station personality
teaches young viewers Bible stories through the use of pictures
and dramatic sketches. Produced by the station. Sunday afternoon; 15 minutes; tape; two cameras; studio origination; one
hour preparation by station; two hours preparation by participants; 30 minutes rehearsal.

Hutchinson, Kansas

TEENARAMA This religious variety show intended for teen-agers
features interviews with outstanding young people, religious
quizzes, choral groups, and discussions of topical subjects. Produced by the station and the Youth for Christ organization. Sunday morning; 30 minutes; tape; two cameras; 90 minutes preparation by station personnel; ten hours preparation by participants;
one hour rehearsal.

Lincoln-Grand Island, Nebraska

F.C.O. (FOR CHILDREN ONLY) During this program station personalities intersperse cartoons with messages to children about attending Sunday School. Sunday morning; one hour; tape, film; two hours preparation by station personnel; one hour preparation by others; 30 minutes rehearsal.

Mayaguez, Puerto Rico

DOCTRINA EN SU HOGAR Intended to give Catholic instruction, *Doctrina En Su Hogar* features 16mm film spots and discussion with children guided by a clergyman. Produced by the Catholic Church. Tuesday afternoon; 30 minutes; live from studio; two cameras; one hour rehearsal.

Midland-Odessa, Texas

TV RELIGION SCHOOL This program, taught by the missionary sisters of Our Lady of Victory, brings young viewers a daily lesson in the Bible. Monday through Friday afternoon; 30 minutes; tape; three cameras; one and one-half hours preparation by station personnel; one hour rehearsal.

New York, New York

LET'S TALK ABOUT GOD Every third Sunday, Maryknoll Sisters present a program for children to illustrate special days on the Roman Catholic calendar. The stories are told in dramatic form, usually with puppets manipulated by the nuns. Sunday morning; 15 minutes; tape; three cameras; six hours preparation by station; 40 hours preparation by participants; three hours rehearsal.

New York, New York

THE BIBLE STORY GAME Children from the New York-New Jersey-Connecticut area participate with the program hosts in a quiz on Biblical subjects. Presented under the auspices of the Protestant Council of the City of New York and the New Jersey Council of Churches. Sunday morning; 15 minutes; tape; three cameras; six hours preparation by station; 25 hours preparation by participants; one and one-half hours rehearsal.

Oklahoma City, Oklahoma
SUNDAY SCHOOL   This Sunday School class, created especially for the child who is a shut-in or who is otherwise "isolated," is taught by a station personality. It is also seen on a station in Fort Worth, Texas. Sunday mornings; 30 minutes; taped in studio; two cameras; three hours preparation by station; one hour rehearsal.

Oklahoma City, Oklahoma
WHAT IS THE WORLD?   A Sunday School program taught jointly by a Catholic and a Protestant, this effort is interfaith in character and interdenominational in content. Sunday morning; 30 minutes; tape; two cameras; four-six hours preparation by the teachers; two-six hours preparation by others; one hour rehearsal.

Omaha, Nebraska
JEAN'S STORY TIME   This Sunday School program presents a hostess who tells stories and teaches her lessons to a live studio audience through the use of puppets. The children's drawings are also exhibited. Produced by the Lutheran Church, but nondenominational in nature.

Portland, Oregon
OBSERVATION SCHOOL—OUR INHERITANCE IN THE CHURCH   The purpose of this program is to explain and demonstrate fundamentals of religious thought through the presentation of actual class situations. Program guides are distributed to religious groups in remote areas so that they can follow the programs and comment upon them. Produced by the station in cooperation with the Children's Work Committee of the Greater Portland Council of Churches. Saturday noon; 30 minutes; tape; two cameras; studio origination; two hours preparation by station personnel; 1 hour rehearsal.

Raleigh, North Carolina
BIBLE STORY TIME   A series of programs of religious stories and songs prepared and performed by people trained in religious education. *Bible Story Time* is produced by the station in conjunction with the Baptist State Convention and with consultation from the Nashville Sunday School Board. Friday morning; eight minutes; tape; two cameras; eight hours preparation by participants; 35 hours preparation by station; three hours rehearsal.

Roswell, New Mexico
BIBLE STORY TIME   In this program, a clergyman speaks to young children, telling them stories from the Bible. Monday afternoon; ten minutes; live from studio.

San Antonio, Texas
TV SUNDAY SCHOOL   This program features Bible stories, songs and prayers in a Sunday School atmosphere. Produced by the station with the Concordia Lutheran Church. Sunday morning; 15 minutes; tape; two cameras; studio origination; one hour preparation by station and four hours by participants; 45 minutes rehearsal.

Spokane, Washington
SUNDAY SCHOOL OF THE AIR   During this weekly program, children selected by various churches in the area sing and read Bible verses. A sermon is also read. The program is designed to appeal to both a general and a children's audience. Sunday morning; 15 minutes; two cameras; 15 minutes rehearsal.

SEASONAL,

HOLIDAY

AND

MEMORIAL

PROGRAMS

CHRIST IN THE CONCRETE CITY
Baltimore, Maryland

This televised version of a contemporary religious drama by
P. W. Turner followed the Passion of Christ from the Thursday in
the Garden of Gethsemane through the Sunday of His rising from
the grave.

The cast of performers was composed of four men and two
women, each of whom played several roles and served also in the
chorus, one person was designated as narrator. An *avant garde*
theatrical technique was used to tell the story, with all props being
mimed or imagined. By re-telling the ancient story in contemporary language, the allusions to life and activities in today's society
were made relevant and unsparingly incisive. In this instance, a
religious drama utilized modern references and techniques to
bring immediacy of the present day to an ancient story. To stress

this aspect of production conception, the program opened with a sequence of special film clips depicting man's failings through current events which was accompanied by narration of the Scriptures on the same subject.

Because of the strong dialogue and pointed contemporary social references the producers expected some adverse public reaction. There was none. Telephone and mail response was almost entirely favorable, and the cast was subsequently asked to repeat their performance throughout the viewing area.

CEREMONY OF THE CAROLS
Cedar Rapids, Iowa

Ceremony of the Carols was a part of an annual Christmas series called "Iowa Sings at Christmas." It featured a 44-voice choir from Clarke College, a Catholic women's college in Dubuque. An announcer from the station's FM classical music service acted as host. The music for the half-hour presentation was the complete work, "A Ceremony of Carols," by Benjamin Britten.

The program was given separate audio and video production. In order to accoustically simulate the qualities of a large church, the choir recorded the selections they were to perform on the program in a nearby high school auditorium. Then the choir recorded the video portion at the station's studio, lip-syncing to the recorded singing.

The final presentation was not visually limited to routine shots of the choir or soloists. The station's production staff equipped a camera with a special effects adaptor which allowed for greater flexibility and creative play with focus. In addition, wood-cuts and other graphic devices were used to illustrate certain musical selections.

The program, one of 15 musical presentations aired by the station during the Christmas season, was videotaped in black and white and presented about two weeks before the holiday.

EYES UPON THE CROSS
Oklahoma City, Oklahoma

The stories of the Bible hold a rich variety of dramatic potentialities, and modern adaptations of them are singularly well-suited to the television medium. *Eyes Upon the Cross*, a 30-minute television adaptation of a play by Don Mueller, made full use of the medium's capacities for presentation of realistic contemporary drama.

The drama concerns a visit with those persons who had gathered to witness the crucifixion of Christ on Calvary. The play was one of several produced by the station's director of religious programming, a minister with experience in religious education.

Tryouts were held for two nights at the college. After two in-studio rehearsals, the program was taped in one day, using three cameras. It was broadcast live in prime time on Good Friday, 1965, and was repeated the following year. The program was produced in association with the drama department of the University of Oklahoma.

A CHILD LOOKS AT CHRISTMAS
Phoenix, Arizona

This half-hour color show depicted the Christmas season as seen through the eyes of a small child. It began with the filmed record of a five-year-old girl's trip through a toy department—a segment in which no words were spoken. Other segments within the program included a drill team of elementary school boys performing to "The March of the Wooden Soldiers."

The final portion of the show was devoted to the telling of an original story relating the events of the Nativity as they might have been viewed by the children of the innkeeper in Bethlehem. The story was pre-taped, with a nine-year-old girl serving as narrator, and was visualized by use of children's art, which had been submitted by grade schools in the area.

CHRISTMAS INTERLUDE
Pittsburgh, Pennsylvania

Television, along with other public media, has frequently been accused of contributing to the "overcommercialization" of the Christmas season. This program set out to demonstrate that a blend of popular secular music and more traditional spiritual music could be combined in good taste to serve the goals of entertainment and serious spiritual expression.

The unusual combination of a string section from the Pittsburgh Symphony, a jazz piano, and an eighty-voice choir helped to bring about this musical message of the spiritual meaning and peacefulness of Christmas. Some of the songs played were "The Twelve Days of Christmas," "Greensleeves," "Snowfall," and "Silent Night."

This program was so pleasing to viewers that it was repeated, by popular demand, one week after its initial telecast.

THE YOUNG SOUND OF CHRISTMAS
San Francisco, California

Community participation is usually an indication of community interest. This is especially true in the case of *The Young Sound of Christmas*. Aired one or two days before Christmas, this annual program presents religious and seasonal musical offerings, performed by young musicians and singers representing Bay Area schools of all grade levels. The participating schools prepare more selections than will be aired, allowing the station the opportunity to use the best efforts of each school. It has become a tradition for viewers and school music educators to include the planning of the show in the school's musical calendar.

The production uses unusual visual effects and special lighting designs to enhance the music. The program is unique in that no narration is used; the music tells its own story. Following the filming of the selections, editors combine the best segments and camera shots into the final program. Several other musical programs of this nature are also presented each year under the series name, *"The Young Sound of Music."*

REJOICE
Terre Haute, Indiana

Religious institutions are sometimes criticized—although to a lesser extent than the television industry itself—for a failure to make effective use of local talent in programming. *Rejoice* represented an imaginative use of local performers in a unique Christmas presentation. More stereotyped choral presentations were rejected in favor of a significant creative effort. The theme of the program revolved around Hugo Distler's "A Rose Is Now Appearing." This selection from *The Christmas Story* led into narrative descriptions and seldom-heard songs of Christmas.

The "rose" theme was executed visually by the use of numerous rose bouquets and individual flowers. Outstanding pieces of religious artwork were also used to illustrate the development of the theme.

In addition to the contribution of the program itself, *Rejoice* also provided an opportunity for a large group of performers to become familiar with television programming procedures.

The program was presented live one week before Christmas. Prime time scheduling made it possible for most area residents to view the presentation. Two cameras; sponsored.

CHRIST IN GLASS
Wilkes-Barre, Pennsylania

Centuries before television could be used to tell visual stories, the use of stained glass to represent Biblical passages was already a high art. *Christ in Glass* combined these ancient and modern media in a beautiful and inspiring presentation. Church windows from the Wilkes-Barre and Scranton area constituted the visual material for this program, which was filmed in color and shown originally on Christmas day, 1965.

A station film crew visited 17 churches (eight Roman Catholic, nine Protestant), and shot footage of windows. Filming took 50 hours and editing, ten hours. When finished, the film was provided with narration, and the show appeared as a presentation of Christmas stories, with the windows visually illustrating the story of the Nativity. The narrator's voice was the only one heard with the exception of three insertions of a choir singing Christmas hymns.

The half-hour program was so well received that it has been repeated by viewers' request.

Seasonal, Holiday and Memorial Programs

Albany, New York

CHRISTMAS EVE MIDNIGHT MASS   The midnight mass offered every Christmas Eve at Albany's Cathedral of the Immaculate Conception is telecast in its entirety. Commentary is written and presented by a priest from Diocesan headquarters. Christmas Eve; two hours; live; five hours rehearsal; 15 hours preparation by Diocesan staff; 15 hours preparation by station.

Atlanta, Georgia

GOOD FRIDAY SERVICE   At noon on Good Friday, seven ministers and laymen present a lesson based on the Seven Stations, with

Easter music bridging the sequences. Good Friday; one hour; tape; two hours rehearsal; 15 hours preparation.

Atlanta, Georgia

EASTER SERVICE CONCERT   Easter music, with vocal arrangements sung by a 400-voice choir, originating from a large theater or stadium. Produced by station personnel. Easter Sunday; tape; three cameras; 100 hours preparation by station personnel; 50 hours preparation by participants; ten hours rehearsal.

Baltimore, Maryland

IN THE SPIRIT OF THE JEWISH NEW YEAR   Commentary on contemporary Jewish life, interwoven with cantorial prayers. Produced by station. Tape; two cameras; studio origination; ten hours preparation by station personnel; ten hours preparation by participants; one hour rehearsal.

Baton Rouge, Louisiana

CHRISTMAS CONCERT   Songs by Louisiana State University's 100-voice choir. Produced by station. Sunday evening; tape; two cameras; originated from Louisiana State University; ten hours preparation by station personnel; ten hours preparation by participants; 15 hours rehearsal.

Colorado Springs, Colorado

CHRISTMAS EVE SERVICES A complete Methodist Christmas Eve service, intended for the shut-in. Produced by station personnel in cooperation with the participating church. Christmas Eve; one hour; live; two cameras; origination from church; four hours preparation by station personnel; four hours preparation by participants.

Colorado Springs, Colorado

CHRISTMAS EVE MIDNIGHT MASS   This Christmas Eve midnight mass, intended for shut-ins, featured a narrator who described the rituals for those who were unfamiliar with the service. Produced by station personnel and participating church. One and one-half hours; live; two cameras; origination from church; six hours preparation by station personnel; four hours preparation by participants.

Columbia, South Carolina

THANKSGIVING DAY SERVICE   Presentation of a half-hour inter-denominational service. Produced by the station. Thanksgiving morning; 30 minutes; tape; three cameras; studio origination; two hours preparation by station personnel; three hours preparation by participants; seven hours rehearsal.

Columbus, Ohio

YOUR LIFE WITH FATHER ROBERT KLEE   A Lenten season series in which Father Klee discusses everyday problems common to people of all faiths. Music is provided by grade school choirs on a rotating basis. Produced by the station with consultation by the Catholic Diocese of Central Ohio. Sunday morning during the Lenten season; half-hour; studio origination; tape; two cameras; two hours preparation by station personnel and eight-ten by others; one hour rehearsal.

Denver, Colorado

CHRISTMAS EVE MASS-ST. JOHN'S EPISCOPAL CHURCH   A complete Christmas Eve Mass intended for shut-ins. 75 minutes; live; three cameras; origination from church; 20 hours preparation by station personnel.

Des Moines, Iowa

THE CRUCIFIXION   Presentation of the story of the Crucifixion in words and music. Produced by station in cooperation with the Council of Churches. Good Friday afternoon; half-hour; live; two cameras; studio origination; four hours preparation by station personnel; four hours preparation by participants; one hour rehearsal.

Des Moines, Iowa

STATIONS OF THE CROSS   A priest reads the Stations of the Cross
while the camera moves from Station to Station. Produced by the
broadcasting personnel with the Chancellor's Office of the Diocese
of Des Moines. Good Friday noon; 30 minutes; studio origination; tape; two cameras; four hours preparation by station personnel; four hours preparation by participants; one hour rehearsal.

Des Moines, Iowa

CHRISTMAS STORY IN DANCE   The story of Christmas was acted in
dance form by the Dieman-Bennett School of Dance. Voice provided by a narrator. December 20, 1964; 30 minutes; tape; two
cameras; studio origination.

Des Moines, Iowa

CHRISTMAS MUSIC   An annual program of four hours of Christmas compositions, performed by nine high school choirs, one college choir, and a local independent choir. Presented during the
week before Christmas. One program per choir; 15–30 minutes;
tape; two cameras; studio origination.

Des Moines, Iowa

CHILDREN'S CHOIRS IN SPECIAL ADVENT   Performances of Christmas music by four children's choirs, for adult listening. The four
choirs are from St. Ludmilla, Bethel AME, First Lutheran
Church and All Saints School. Sunday afternoons; approximately
15 minutes; tape; two cameras; studio origination.

Detroit, Michigan

EASTER MASS/CHRISTMAS MASS   An annual presentation (since
1947) of an Easter morning mass and a Christmas midnight mass.
Produced by station personnel in cooperation with the Archdiocese of Detroit. Easter Sunday morning and Christmas Eve;
length varies; live; three cameras.

Detroit, Michigan
PASSOVER, CHANUKAH, ROSH HASHANA An annual series, presented since 1947, these dramatic programs celebrate the Jewish
High Holy Days. Produced by the station and the Jewish Community Council. The writers and talent, provided by the Council,
aim to acquaint viewers with the tenets of the Jewish religion.
Day of week varies; 30 minutes; tape; two or three cameras; one
and one-half hours rehearsal.

Detroit, Michigan
EASTER SUNDAY SERVICE A presentation of the Easter Sunday
service from the Episcopal Church. Primarily intended for shut-
ins. Sunday morning; one hour; live; three cameras; half-hour
rehearsal; two hours preparation by station personnel.

Detroit, Michigan
LUTHERAN TRE ORE SERVICE An annual presentation of the
service held in Lutheran churches on Good Friday. Produced by
station personnel and the Missouri Synod of Greater Detroit. Friday afternoon; one hour; live; three cameras; three hours rehearsal; four hours preparation by station personnel.

Detroit, Michigan
THANKSGIVING SUNDAY SERVICE An annual presentation of the
"Ingathering" Thanksgiving Sunday service at the First Baptist
Church of Birmingham, Michigan. Origination from the church;
Sunday; one hour; live; three cameras; one hour rehearsal; two
hours preparation by station personnel.

Detroit, Michigan
THE CALL OF THE SPIRIT An annual program explaining the
significance of the Jewish Day of Atonement, Yom Kippur. To
acquaint viewers of all faiths with the religious and historical importance of this Jewish holy day, two rabbis from the Jewish
Community Council discuss the meaning and history of the day,

and chant from the Torah. Sunday; 30 minutes; two cameras; one hour rehearsal; two hours preparation by station personnel.

Grand Rapids, Michigan

PORTRAIT OF THE PASSION   An annual program which describes the Passion of Christ through narration, music, and original works of art. Local artists' work, including non-objective paintings, is used to tell the familiar story in a new way. Produced in cooperation with the annual Christian Art Show sponsored by the Peace Lutheran Church of Sparta, Michigan. Narration and music by a local clergyman and a parochial school choir. Taped; Sunday afternoon; 30 minutes; two cameras; one hour rehearsal; 14 hours preparation by station personnel; 20–25 hours preparation by participants.

Grand Rapids, Michigan

SALVATION ARMY EASTER FASHION SHOW   An annual display of little girls' fashions contributed to the Salvation Army for distribution to needy youngsters. Judges select prize-winning fashions from the entries of seamstresses who make and contribute clothing for Easter-time distribution. Produced by the station with the Salvation Army. Easter Sunday afternoon; 30 minutes; live; three cameras; one hour rehearsal; 18–20 hours preparation by station; four-six hours preparation by participants.

Grand Rapids, Michigan

COMMUNITY CHRISTMAS CARD   An annual series of five programs of Christmas music. Seven high schools and three colleges provide the musical talent. Produced by the station with the support of the local Council of Churches. Broadcast on five weekday mornings preceding Christmas; 30 minutes; tape; two cameras; half-hour rehearsal; four hours preparation by station personnel.

Hartford, Connecticut

LAYMAN'S WAY OF THE CROSS   An annual program in which twelve prominent laymen recite the Stations of the Cross. Produced by broadcasters in association with the Roman Catholic

Archdiocese of Hartford. Friday afternoon, once yearly; 30 minutes; live from studio; three cameras; one hour rehearsal; eight hours preparation by station; one and one-half hours preparation by others.

Hershey, Pennsylvania
PORTRAIT OF CHRISTMAS This program expresses the spirit of the Christmas holiday through expressions of music and art. As many as 120 pieces of nativity art have been shown. Produced by station. Evenings of December 23rd and 24th; 30 minutes; tape; three cameras; studio origination; 50 hours preparation by station personnel; four hours preparation by participants; six hours rehearsal.

Knoxville, Tennessee
JEWISH HIGH HOLY DAYS An annual dramatization of the celebration of Rosh Hashana on the eve of the Jewish New Year by the rabbi and members of Knoxville's Heska Amuna Congregation. Intended to be informative for both the Jewish and Christian members of the audience. Once a year; 30 minutes; tape and live; three cameras; one hour rehearsal; three hours preparation by station personnel.

Knoxville, Tennessee
SOUNDS OF CHRISTMAS An annual presentation of song, music, and the Nativity Play by the Knoxville College Choir, the Maryville College Madrigal Singers and children from the First Baptist Church of Gatlinburg, Tennessee. Christmas afternoon; one and one-half hours; tape and live; three cameras; five hours rehearsal; five hours preparation by station personnel.

Lafayette, Louisiana
MIDNIGHT MASS A complete Christmas Eve midnight Mass, intended for the shut-in. Produced by station. Christmas Eve; 90 minutes; live; two cameras.

Los Angeles, California
HOLLYWOOD BOWL EASTER SUNRISE SERVICES   An annual presentation, started about 15 years ago, of Easter morning services from the Hollywood Bowl. Station produces the telecast in cooperation with the Hollywood Bowl Association. Program features musical groups who render hymns, religious readings by well-known actors and actresses, and a sermon by a prominent minister. One hour; live and tape; four cameras; 150 hours of preparation by station personnel; four-five hours of rehearsal.

Mason City, Iowa
LUTHERAN REFORMATION SUNDAY PROGRAM   Presented on Reformation Sunday, this program features choir selections followed by a sermon. Produced by station personnel with Lutheran ministers and the Waldorf College Choir. Reformation Sunday night; half-hour; live; two cameras; studio origination; two hours preparation by station personnel; one hour rehearsal.

Mason City, Iowa
WALDORF COLLEGE CHOIR   Scheduled during the Christmas and Easter seasons, this program features short inspirational messages and religious music by the Waldorf College Choir. Produced by station personnel and the Waldorf College Choir. 30 minutes; live; two cameras; studio origination; one and one-half hours preparation by station staff.

Mobile, Alabama
EASTER SUNRISE SERVICE   Since 1958 this program has featured the annual outdoor Easter Sunrise service of the Broad Street Presbyterian Church. The service includes participation by the choir, local clergy, and a visiting speaker. 75 minutes; live; two cameras; four hours preparation by station.

Mobile, Alabama
MIDNIGHT MASS   A Christmas Eve midnight Mass has been presented annually since 1960. Live; two cameras.

Mobile, Alabama

FEAST OF CHRIST THE KING   This annual program features a parade in which most Roman Catholic adult groups and children from all parochial schools march. A sermon is given by the Bishop of the Diocese of Mobile and Birmingham at Municipal Auditorium. October 31; 30 minutes; live; two cameras; four hours preparation.

New Orleans, Louisiana

MIDNIGHT MASS   Since 1949 this program has presented the Solemn High Mass service which originates from the Basilica of St. Louis in New Orleans, celebrated by the Archbishop of New Orleans. Midnight at Christmas; until conclusion; live; three cameras.

Oakland-San Francisco

SONG OF TRIUMPH   Program consisted of a chorus and a 30-piece orchestra in a joint presentation of a contemporary Easter cantata. Produced by the station with the cooperation of the San Jose First Baptist Church. Live; half-hour; three cameras; two and a half hours rehearsal; 15 hours preparation by station.

Oakland-San Francisco, California

CHRISTMAS CHORALIERS   The Peninsula Choraliers were presented in various settings with emphasis on the religious aspect of modern Christmas songs. December 23; 30 minutes; tape; two cameras; three hours rehearsal; 22 hours preparation by station.

Oklahoma City, Oklahoma

THE THREE BEGGARS   Talent from Oklahoma City University performed the traditional Christmas story of *The Three Beggars*. Produced by station with the Music and Drama Departments of Oklahoma City University. Christmas Eve; half-hour; tape; three cameras; studio origination; 20 hours preparation by participants; six hours rehearsal.

Pasco, Washington
PENTECOST SUNDAY   In this discussion program several ministers explained the meaning of Pentecost Sunday. Produced by station personnel. Sunday afternoon; tape; two cameras; studio origination; three hours preparation by station personnel; five hours preparation by participants.

Peoria, Illinois
CHANUKAH OBSERVANCE   The highlights of this important Jewish holiday were presented in this program, produced by station personnel in cooperation with Agudas Achim Synagogue. Sunday afternoon; 30 minutes; tape; three cameras; 20 hours rehearsal; 50 hours preparation by station; 50 hours by others.

Phoenix, Arizona
CHRISTMAS WITH THE CANTERBURY SINGERS   This was a Christmas season program in which the Canterbury Singers, a choral group from Phoenix College, sang songs and told stories about the holiday. December 22; tape; three cameras; studio origination; 120 hours preparation by station personnel; six hours rehearsal.

Phoenix, Arizona
WELCOME YULE   In this religious variety show the Phoenix Boys Choir, supported by visual aids and pertinent narration, brought the flavor of the Yule season to the viewer. Produced by the station. Afternoon of December 21st, 1964; 30 minutes; tape; three cameras; studio origination; 100 hours preparation by station; 40 hours rehearsal.

Phoenix, Arizona
AND THE WORLD REJOICED   This program explained the story of the Nativity and the spread of Christianity by the use of prose and songs. Famous paintings of religious scenes were used to enhance the narrative. Produced by station; Christmas afternoon; 30 minutes; tape; three cameras; studio origination; 200 hours preparation by station; 40 hours rehearsal.

Pittsburgh, Pennsylvania
STATIONS OF THE CROSS; GOOD FRIDAY SERVICE These programs, which alternate annually, are produced with the cooperation of the Catholic Diocese of Pittsburgh and the Pittsburgh Council of Churches respectively. The former presents a Catholic chaplain explaining the Stations of the Cross and delivering a brief sermon. Afternoon of Good Friday; 30 minutes; tape; two cameras; one hour rehearsal; 15 hours preparation by station personnel; eight hours preparation by others.

Portland, Oregon
CHRISTMAS—1965. Through the use of films, dancing, acting, choirs and pertinent narration, this variety show sought to express the meaning of the holiday. Produced by station personnel and the Commission of Worship and Fine Arts of the Greater Portland Council of Churches. Sunday morning; originated at various locations; 30 minutes; tape and film; one camera; two days preparation; one hour rehearsal.

Rockford, Illinois
SONGS FOR CHRISTMAS This program features Christmas music in the form of five minute choral presentations by each of eleven participating choirs. Produced by station personnel. Christmas season; mornings; five minutes; tape; three cameras; studio origination; 30 minutes preparation by station; 15 minutes rehearsal.

Rockford, Illinois
CHURCH SERVICES ON EASTER, THANKSGIVING, AND CHRISTMAS SUNDAYS This series presents programs consisting of Easter service from the Second Congregational Church and Thanksgiving-Christmas Sunday services from the Court Street Methodist Church. Produced by station in cooperation with the participating pastor. Holiday Sundays; one hour; live; remote; three cameras; ten hours preparation by station.

San Antonio, Texas
SPECIAL CHRISTMAS AND EASTER PROGRAMS   Annual half-hour
programs of cantatas are aired during the Christmas and Easter
seasons. 30 minutes; taped; studio origination; three cameras; one
hour rehearsal; five hours of preparation by station; 30 hours by
others.

San Antonio, Texas
NIGHT OF ECUMENICAL WITNESS   This annual broadcast presents
combined Protestant and Roman Catholic services from the Municipal Auditorium. Produced by the station and the participating clergy. Sunday morning; one hour; tape; three cameras.

San Francisco, California
THE MESSIAH   The program presented a performance of portions
of Handel's "The Messiah," originally produced by the Reorgan-
ized Church of Jesus Christ of the Latter Day Saints in Kansas
City. Produced by station personnel in cooperation with the
church. Sunday morning; one hour; tape.

San Francisco, California
GETHSEMANE   A performance of an original verse cantata dealing with the beauty of Easter, and illustrated by 15th and 16th-
century engravings, was presented by members of the Concert Ensemble of the San Francisco Lyric Theater, under the direction of
William Siden, and by the San Francisco Baroque Ensemble,
under the direction of Ericka-Marie Hoilet. Produced by the station. Sunday afternoon; one hour; tape; studio origination.

San Francisco, California
HIGH HOLY DAYS   This broadcast included Jewish New Year
services and a commentary on the history of the ceremony. Produced by the station with the participating rabbi, cantor, and
congregation, this program was designed to give viewers of all
faiths a better understanding of Jewish practices. September 26;
30 minutes; tape; three cameras; studio origination; 24 hours

preparation by station personnel; twelve hours preparation by participants; four hours rehearsal.

Scranton, Pennsylvania
SONGS OF EMANUEL   An annual concert of Christmas music. Produced by the station and the Choir of St. Ann's Monastery. Christmas Day; 30 minutes; studio origination; tape; three cameras; two hours rehearsal; ten hours preparation by station; ten hours preparation by others.

South Bend, Indiana
LENTEN DEVOTIONS   This program, seen during the Lenten season, featured five-minute sermons and prayers by members of the local clergy selected by the Council of Churches. Produced by station in cooperation with the St. Joseph County Council of Churches. Twice daily, Monday-Friday mornings during Lent; five minutes; tape; two cameras; studio origination.

Springfield, Massachusetts
GOOD FRIDAY SERVICE   This annual program presents sermons, Bible readings and religious music. Produced by the Radio-TV Director of the Diocese of Springfield. Good Friday noon; three hours; live; two cameras; three hours rehearsal; three hours preparation by station personnel; 20 hours preparation by others.

Terre Haute, Indiana
GOOD FRIDAY VESPERS AND CHRISTMAS VESPERS   Combining sermons, Scriptural readings and musical selections, these yearly programs demonstrate cooperation between the Protestant and Catholic clergy. Vocalists and performers not generally heard on television provide music appropriate to the season. Produced by the station with the Terre Haute Council of Churches, Catholic Council of Men, community clergymen and the music departments of colleges and universities. Good Friday and Christmas Day, mid-afternoon; 30 minutes; two cameras; one hour of rehearsal; 15 hours of preparation by the station; ten hours by others.

Visalia, California
ST. JAMES CHRISTMAS MASS   This program is a Christmas Mass intended especially for shut-ins. Produced by the station. Christmas morning; two hours; live; three cameras; originated from the church; eight hours preparation by station personnel.

Washington, D. C.
LESSONS AND FIVE CAROLS   The story of Christ was told by five readers with the support of five choirs provided by the National Cathedral under the direction of R. Wayne Dirksen. Produced by the station. Christmas Eve; one hour; tape; twelve hours of rehearsal; four cameras; 20 hours of preparation by station personnel; 100 hours by others.

Youngstown, Ohio
THE LORD IS MY SHEPHERD   This year-round program presents the background of the days of important observances celebrated by the major faiths through narration and pictures. Produced by station. Five minutes; live; tape, film, stills; two cameras; studio origination; five to ten hours preparation by station personnel; 30 minutes rehearsal.

Youngstown, Ohio
EASTER BYZANTINE MASS   On Easter Sunday a complete Byzantine Mass was telecast. Produced by station with participating priests. Easter Sunday; one hour; live and tape; three cameras; studio origination; ten hours preparation by station personnel; five hours preparation by participants; two hours rehearsal.

Yuma, Arizona
CHRISTMAS IN STORY AND SONG   This program featured Christmas music and songs by the Yuma Concert Chorale, with special narration and visuals. Produced by station personnel in cooperation with the participants. Monday evening; one hour; tape; two cameras; studio originated; three hours preparation by station personnel; two hours rehearsal.

PROGRAMS OF

WORSHIP,

INSPIRATION

AND MEDITATION

SEVEN DAYS OF DECISION
Ardmore, Oklahoma

Television's capacity for reaching great numbers of people holds a natural attraction for those who wish to spread the message of the Gospel. This situation led to the creation of *Seven Days of Decision,* a week long crusade presented by the Churches of Christ in South Oklahoma and North Texas.

Television expanded the crusade's coverage during five of the seven nights, Monday through Friday, by telecasting it in prime time. Each program was planned for an hour, but on the final evening of the crusade an additional 30 minutes of time was requested in order that the baptism of a new convert could be televised.

The general public responded favorably, and the congregations presenting the series were high in their praise of the value of a televised crusade. As a result, further TV coverage is planned.

SERMONS IN SONG
Corpus Christi, Texas

Religious songs, prayers, and inspirational thoughts are combined in this weekly 15-minute program, broadcast on Sunday afternoon. A 35-voice choir provides much of the musical content, and two selections are provided by either guest soloist, trio or quartet.

The program host, pastor of the First Assembly of God Church, offers a prayer, reads from the Scriptures and closes the program with an inspirational thought. The pastor has expressed his opinion regarding the use of television by religious institutions in this way: "The most exciting, challenging, and rewarding efforts of my years of ministry have come as a result of television. One must not ignore this medium that has so drastically influenced the world in recent years. Since we believe in 'being anchored to the rock and geared to the time' we implement our convictions by television participation."

Four programs are produced at each monthly video-taping session. The program is sponsored; the sponsoring firms receive only a brief credit at the opening and conclusion of the program. Despite competition from football games on the other channels, the station reports excellent viewer reaction, particularly from shut-ins in the area.

SERVICIOS RELIGIOSOS EN ESPAÑOL
(RELIGIOUS SERVICES IN SPANISH)
Corpus Christi, Texas

Since approximately fifty percent of the population in the area is Latin American, and many of the citizens do not speak English fluently, the community appeal of this program is obvious. *Reli-*

gious Services In Spanish has additional impact because it invites Spanish speaking congregations of all denominations in the area to participate.

In order to give the program a sense of continuity, each congregation appears for one month, or four successive programs. This allows the pastor or preacher to develop a continuing theme for his series of programs.

The program introduced in Spanish by a station announcer, begins with a musical selection provided by the church which cooperates in the production of the program. The pastor of the church then delivers a short sermon or inspirational message. A vocal or instrumental selection concludes the program.

THE SINGING NUNS OF
SAINT MARY-OF-THE-WOODS
Terre Haute, Indiana

This program featured a half-hour concert by the Providence Sisters' Choir of Saint Mary-of-the-Woods. The choir is composed of aspirants, novices, and juniorate nuns of the Sisters of Providence. With the exceptions of a high school concert, the group had never appeared in public before this first experience with television. The "new look" in the Catholic Church—not evident to a marked degree in 1964—was clearly demonstrated in this program, especially by the choir's folk-style rendition of "Blowin' in the Wind." At the time of the telecast, this modern touch was unique.

In addition to the musical presentation by the choir, the program included a brief filmed segment, shot at the novitiate, which illustrated the daily lives of the young women in the choir. The filmed segment was valuable in itself because it offered a rare and candid look at convent life. The joy of the young women was evident not only in their songs, but in their lives as well.

The videotaped program was a half-hour long, and was first

presented on a Sunday morning. Later, to mark the 125th anniversary of the Sisters of Providence, the program was repeated during prime evening hours as a public affairs production.

THE GOSPEL ACCORDING TO THE FOLK SINGER
Wichita Falls, Texas

By combining the words of the Gospel and the language of the folk song, this five-minute program expanded the language of the Gospel through the vernacular of present-day language.

The simple format resulted in a meaningful religious experience for the viewer. The opening of the program highlighted a minister seated on a high stool before a title background slide of the show's title. After a brief introduction of guitar music and religious chords, the announcer introduced the minister who read a short passage from one of the Gospels. Then he said: "Through the years the eternal message of this text has been passed on from generation to generation by word of mouth, through story and song, from the Madrigal Singers of England to the hill people of Tennessee; and through the idiom of the folk singer it comes out like this. . . ." The second camera cut to the folk singer, who sang a song based on the particular Biblical text. At the conclusion of the folk song the minister drew the Biblical text and the vernacular text together in a brief, but relevant message.

The Television Service

Baltimore, Maryland
SUNDAY SERMON   A weekly Protestant service produced by the station in cooperation with the Maryland Council of Churches. Sunday morning; 30 minutes; tape; two cameras; two hours preparation by station; one and one-half hours preparation by participating church; one hour rehearsal.

Cincinnati, Ohio

CHURCH BY THE SIDE OF THE ROAD   This is a condensed Protestant service that began on radio in 1923 and on television in 1948. The services are made interdenominational in character by using a different minister and choir each week. Sunday morning; 30 minutes; tape; two cameras; one hour rehearsal.

Columbia, South Carolina

SOUTH CAROLINA TELEVISION PULPIT   Local churches and synagogues, participating on a rotating basis, present half-hour Sunday services. Produced by station. Sunday, 9 and 11 A.M.; 30 minutes; tape; three cameras; studio origination; three hours preparation by station; four hours preparation by participants; 30 minutes rehearsal.

Columbus, Ohio

CHURCH BY THE SIDE OF THE ROAD   This program, intended for the viewer unable to attend church, presents a complete Protestant service. Produced by the station. Sunday morning; 30 minutes; tape; two cameras; studio origination; 30 minutes preparation by station; two hours preparation by participants; one hour rehearsal.

Davenport, Iowa

SUNDAY MORNING WORSHIP   Local area pastors, choirs and Sunday School teachers appear on this program which offers a shortened church service. Produced by the station and the Council of Churches in consultation with its Director for Rock Island and Scott County. Film inserts are used for special religious holidays or weeks. Sunday; 30 minutes; taped in studio; two or three cameras; one hour rehearsal.

Des Moines, Iowa

CENTRAL IOWA CHURCH OF THE AIR   This shortened church service features filmed scenes of a church interior which are shown at the opening and closing of the ceremony. Produced by the station with the Des Moines Area Council and Iowa Council of Churches. Sunday morning; 30 minutes; tape and film; two cameras; studio origination; 30 minutes preparation by station; two hours preparation by participants; one hour rehearsal.

Fort Worth, Texas

Fort Worth Council of Churches This church service, intended for shut-ins, includes a choir and sermon. Produced by the station in cooperation with the Fort Worth Council of Churches. Sunday morning; 30 minutes; tape; two cameras; studio origination; 90 minutes preparation by station personnel; 30 minutes rehearsal.

Greenville, North Carolina

Light Unto My Path A minister conducts services and delivers a sermon on this program especially produced for the deaf. Produced by the North Carolina Baptist State Convention. Sunday morning; tape; two cameras; studio origination.

High Point, North Carolina

TV Pulpit This complete church service is presented for viewers who are bed-ridden or who live in remote areas. Sunday morning; 30 minutes; tape; two cameras; studio origination; twelve hours preparation by station; one hour rehearsal.

Huntington, West Virginia

TV Chapel A minister selected by the local ministerial association appears on this program to conduct services and deliver a sermon. Produced by the station in cooperation with the participating church. Sunday, noon; 30 minutes; tape; two cameras; studio origination; one hour preparation by station; one hour rehearsal.

Jacksonville, Florida

Together We Worship Local houses of worship representing the major faiths present half-hour services on a weekly rotating basis. Produced by the station. Sunday morning; 30 minutes; tape; two cameras; studio origination; 30 minutes rehearsal.

Kansas city, Missouri
YOUR CHURCH AND MINE   By presenting the religious services of various churches, this series attempts to illustrate the similarities between houses of worship and to show how different faiths work toward the same goal. Produced by the station and the Council of Churches, with the cooperation of the Catholic Diocese of Kansas City-St. Joseph. Sunday morning; 30 minutes; two or three cameras; taped in studio; ten hours preparation by station; 20 hours preparation by others; 90 minute rehearsal.

Lexington, Kentucky
MIDWAY BAPTIST HOUR   A typical church service is presented from the studio by the minister and choir of the Midway Baptist Church. Sunday; 30 minutes; live; one camera; one hour preparation by station; 30 minute rehearsal.

Little Rock, Arkansas
SUNDAY CHURCH SERVICE   A condensed version of a different church service is presented each week. Produced in cooperation with the participating churches. Sunday morning; 30 minutes; taped in studio; five hours preparation by station; two cameras; one hour rehearsal.

Memphis, Tennessee
CHRIST IS THE ANSWER   This program offers a shortened version of a church service consisting of music and a sermon. Produced by the station and the church. Sunday morning; 30 minutes; tape; three cameras; studio origination; one hour preparation by station; three hours preparation by participants; one hour rehearsal.

Miami, Florida
PROTESTANT WORSHIP HOUR   Intended for people who cannot attend their own churches, this program follows the pattern of a regular Protestant service: Scriptures, hymn, prayer, choral re-

sponse and a sermon by a different guest pastor each week. Sunday morning; 30 minutes preparation by the station; 30 minutes rehearsal.

Miami, Florida
JEWISH WORSHIP HOUR   A rabbi and cantor, selected by the Rabbinical Association of Greater Miami, present prayers, Scripture and a sermon. Sunday morning; 30 minutes; tape; two cameras; 30 minutes preparation by station; 30 minutes rehearsal.

Mobile, Alabama
HOUR OF PENTECOSTAL POWER   The elements of this program are hymns sung by the choir, church announcements and a sermon—all presented by the Prichard Assembly of God Church. Sunday morning; 30 minutes; tape; two cameras; 20 minutes rehearsal.

New Bern, North Carolina
SUNDAY WORSHIP   Area churches, represented by their minister and choir, alternate in presenting programs of sermons, music and choir selections, primarily intended for bed-ridden people and others who are unable to attend church. Produced by the station in association with the New Bern Ministerial Association and the Eastern Carolina Diocese. Sunday noon; 30 minutes; live and tape; two cameras; 30 minutes rehearsal; two hours preparation by station; four hours by others.

Norfolk, Virginia
HOUSE OF WORSHIP   During this program, which is especially intended for viewers unable to attend services, a different church presents hymns, Scripture, prayers and a sermon each week. Produced by the station. Sunday morning; 30 minutes; tape; three cameras; studio origination; two hours preparation by station; two hours preparation by participants; 90 minutes rehearsal.

Odessa, Texas
MORNING WORSHIP Participating on an alternating basis, churches of different denominations present morning services

each Sunday. Produced by the station with the participating church. 30 minutes; tape; two cameras; studio origination; one hour preparation by station.

Oklahoma City, Oklahoma
SUNDAY MORNING WORSHIP   Services primarily intended for shut-ins are presented by a different church each week. Ministers and the choirs of the several churches, under the aegis of the Greater Oklahoma City Council of Churches, are the program participants. Sunday morning; 30 minutes; tape; two cameras; two to four hours preparation by non-station personnel; 30 minutes rehearsal.

Oklahoma City, Oklahoma
OKLAHOMA CITY AT WORSHIP   Participating churches selected by the Oklahoma City Council of Churches alternate in providing typical half-hour services. Produced by the station. Sunday morning; 30 minutes; taped in studio; two cameras; four hours preparation by station; three to four hours rehearsal.

Pittsburgh, Pennsylvania
CHAPEL ON THE HILL   This program consists of a condensed religious service conducted by host clergy and choirs. Produced by the station in cooperation with the Council of Churches of the Pittsburgh area. Sunday morning; 30 minutes; tape; three cameras; studio origination; two hours preparation by station; three days preparation by participants; one hour rehearsal.

Raleigh, North Carolina
LIGHT UNTO MY PATH   This program presents music, a Bible lesson and sermon. Interpreters translate the Bible lesson and sermon into sign-language for the deaf viewers. The program is available on tape to any television station requesting it; it is carried by 18 stations in eight southern and border states. Produced by the station with the Baptist State Convention. Sunday morning; one hour; tape; three cameras; 20 hours preparation by participants; six hours preparation by station; two hours rehearsal.

Roanoke, Virginia

TV CHAPEL   Members of the Roanoke Ministers' Conference alternate weekly in presenting a short church service. Sunday noon; 30 minutes; tape; two cameras; eight hours preparation; one hour rehearsal.

Roanoke, Virginia

VOICE OF ELIM   This abridged Sunday service is prepared and presented by the minister of the Baptist Church. Sunday morning; 30 minutes; tape.

Rockford, Illinois

SUNDAY SERVICE   Each program in this weekly series presents an abbreviated church service which usually includes a choir. Produced by station personnel and the Rockford Ministerial Association. Sunday morning; 30 minutes; tape; three cameras; studio origination; 15 minutes preparation by station; 30 minutes rehearsal.

Temple-Waco, Texas

LIGHT OF THE WORLD   Members of the Waco and Temple Ministerial Alliances take turns in presenting condensed church services. Produced by the station. Sunday morning; 30 minutes; taped in studio; 14 hours preparation; two cameras; one hour rehearsal.

Toledo, Ohio

SUNDAY SANCTUARY   A minister and choir, provided by the radio-TV committee of the Council of Churches, present abbreviated worship services and a sermonette of ten or twelve minutes in this program. Sunday morning; 30 minutes; taped in studio; two cameras; 30 minutes rehearsal.

The Church Service in the Studio

Alexandria, Minnesota
CATHOLIC HOUR   The celebration of a Mass, especially intended for shut-ins. Produced by the station with the cooperation of the St. Cloud-Minnesota Catholic Diocese. Sunday morning; 30 minutes; live; origination from studio; three-five hours preparation by participants; two cameras; 30 minute rehearsal.

Anchorage, Alaska
FIRST BAPTIST CHURCH   A complete Baptist service produced live by the station in cooperation with the church. Sunday morning; one hour; live; two cameras; six hours preparation by the station.

Atlanta, Georgia
CHURCH OF THE WEEK   Each week a different minister and choir present the equivalent of a regular church service. The Greater Atlanta Council of Churches serves as the coordinating agent. Sunday morning; one hour; tape; two cameras.

Buffalo, New York
THE HOLY SACRIFICE OF THE MASS   Seminarians from St. John Vienney Seminary say Mass from a specially built Liturgical Altar, which is installed in the studio. The program is coordinated by a Monsignor of the Catholic Diocese of Buffalo. Sunday morning; 30 minutes; live from studio; two cameras; six hours preparation by station.

Burlington, Vermont
THE MASS   This program presents a complete Catholic Mass. Produced live by the station. Sunday morning; 45 minutes; two cameras; live, studio origination; 16 hours preparation by participants; 30 minutes rehearsal.

Similar services, involving the presentation of all elements of the full church service, are conducted in the following cities:

Chicago, Illinois
MASS FOR SHUT-INS

Columbus, Ohio
THE CATHOLIC MASS

Detroit, Michigan
MASS FOR SHUT-INS

Grand Rapids, Michigan
HOLY SACRIFICE OF THE MASS

Grand Rapids, Michigan
WOODLAND CHAPEL (Protestant)

Green Bay, Wisconsin
SUNDAY MASS

Lake Charles, Louisiana
TRINITY BAPTIST CHURCH

Los Angeles, California
CHURCH IN THE HOME (Ecumenical)

Miami, Florida
MASS FOR SHUT-INS

Milwaukee, Wisconsin
SUNDAY MORNING WORSHIP (Ecumenical)

Milwaukee, Wisconsin
MASS FOR SHUT-INS

New Bedford, Massachusetts
TV MASS

New Bedford, Massachusetts
WORSHIP (Protestant)

New Bedford, Massachusetts
FAITH OF OUR FATHERS (Jewish)

New Britain, Connecticut
SACRIFICE OF THE MASS

New Orleans, Louisiana
HOLY MASS

Omaha, Nebraska
MASS FOR SHUT-INS

Paducah, Kentucky
PADUCAH DEVOTION (Ecumenical)

Phoenix, Arizona
MASS FOR SHUT-INS

Portsmouth, Virginia
SUNDAY MORNING CHURCH SERVICE (Ecumenical)

Roanoke, Virginia
TV SUNDAY SERVICE (Baptist, Methodist, Presbyterian, Lutheran)

St. Louis, Missouri
CATHOLIC MASS

South Bend, Indiana
THE HOLY SACRIFICE OF THE MASS

Springfield, Massachusetts
CHALICE OF SALVATION (Catholic)

Washington, D. C.
Mass for Shut-Ins

Services from the Church

Ada, Oklahoma
The First Baptist Church Service   This full service includes music, a sermon, invitation, meditation and congregational singing. Sunday morning; one hour; live, remote from the church; one camera.

Amarillo, Texas
Church Services   A local church service is conducted, followed by a short sermon. Produced by the station in cooperation with the participating church. Sunday morning; one hour; live; two cameras; originated from the church; three and one half hours preparation by the station.

Ardmore, Oklahoma
First Baptist Church   This weekly program, which is under the control of the church, presents a live service. It is broadcast from the church using the church's equipment. Sunday morning; one hour; live, remote; three cameras; one half hour preparation by station; three hours preparation by others.

Atlanta, Georgia
Services from First Baptist Church   These services are broadcast live from the church sanctuary and are conducted by one of Atlanta's best-known ministers. Sunday morning; one hour; live, remote; two cameras; four hours preparation by station.

Austin, Texas
Sunday Morning Worship Services   This program presents services from the Hyde Park Baptist Church, Christo Rey Catholic Church, United Presbyterian Church and St. Paul Lutheran Church on a weekly rotating basis. Produced by the station and

the participating church. Sunday morning; one hour; live, remote from church; two cameras; two and one half hours preparation by the station.

Similar remote broadcasts, originated at the house of worship, are presented in the following cities:

Bakersfield, California
FIRST BAPTIST CHURCH SUNDAY MORNING SERVICE

Baton Rouge, Louisiana
FIRST BAPTIST CHURCH

Bryan, Texas
CHURCH SERVICE

Charleston, South Carolina
CITADEL SQUARE BAPTIST CHURCH SERVICE

Charlotte, North Carolina
FIRST PRESBYTERIAN CHURCH

Chicago, Illinois
CHICAGOLAND CHURCH HOUR (PROTESTANT)

Cleveland, Ohio
MASS FOR SHUT-INS

Colorado Springs, Colorado
FIRST METHODIST CHURCH

Columbia, South Carolina
FIRST BAPTIST CHURCH SERVICE

Columbus, Georgia
FIRST BAPTIST CHURCH SERVICES

Columbus, Georgia
FIRST PRESBYTERIAN CHURCH SERVICE

Dallas, Texas
HIGHLAND PARK PRESBYTERIAN AND HIGHLAND PARK METHODIST CHURCH SERVICES

Dallas, Texas
HOUR OF WORHSIP (Ecumenical)

Decatur, Alabama
CENTRAL BAPTIST HOUR

Denver, Colorado
CALVARY TEMPLE HOUR

El Dorado, Arkansas-Monroe, Louisiana
FIRST BAPTIST CHURCH

El Paso, Texas
FIRST BAPTIST CHURCH SERVICE

Evansville, Indiana
ST. MARK'S LUTHERAN CHURCH WORSHIP SERVICE

Fort Worth, Texas
FIRST BAPTIST CHURCH OF DALLAS

Fort Worth, Texas
MORNING CHURCH SERVICE   (Ecumenical)

Houston, Texas
FIRST METHODIST CHURCH

Houston, Texas
ST. LUKE'S METHODIST SERVICE

Houston, Texas
SOUTH MAIN BAPTIST SERVICE

Hutchinson, Kansas
INVITATION TO WORSHIP   (Protestant)

Jackson, Mississippi
FIRST BAPTIST CHURCH SERVICE

Jackson, Mississippi
FIRST PRESBYTERIAN CHURCH

Jacksonville, Florida
SOUTH JACKSONVILLE PRESBYTERIAN CHURCH SERVICE

Knoxville, Tennessee
SUNDAY MORNING WORSHIP SERVICE   (Ecumenical)

Little Rock-Pine Bluff, Arkansas
SERVICE   (Baptist)

Memphis, Tennessee
BELLEVUE BAPTIST CHURCH

Midland-Odessa, Texas
FIRST BAPTIST CHURCH SERVICES

Minneapolis, Minnesota
SUNDAY CHURCH REMOTE

Montgomery, Alabama
LOCAL CHURCH SERVICE   (Methodist and Baptist)

Odessa, Texas
FIRST BAPTIST CHURCH SERVICES

Omaha, Nebraska
SERVICES FROM KOUNTZE MEMORIAL CHURCH

Port Arthur, Texas
FIRST BAPTIST CHURCH OF BEAUMONT

Roanoke, Virginia
SUNDAY CHURCH SERVICE   (Ecumenical)

San Jose, California
SOLEMN HIGH PONTIFICAL MASS

Seattle, Washington
MORNING WORSHIP

Shreveport, Louisiana
HOUR OF WORSHIP   (Protestant)

Sioux Falls, South Dakota
WEEK OF PRAYER   (Ecumenical)

Spartanburg, South Carolina
FIRST BAPTIST CHURCH SERVICE

Springfield, Missouri
HIGH STREET BAPTIST CHURCH WORSHIP SERVICE

Sweetwater, Texas
UNIVERSITY BAPTIST CHURCH

Tallahassee-Thomasville, Florida
FIRST BAPTIST CHURCH SERVICES

Tulsa, Oklahoma
SUNDAY WORSHIP   (Protestant)

Tulsa, Oklahoma
CHURCH SERVICES   (Protestant)

Wichita Falls, Texas
FIRST BAPTIST CHURCH SERVICE

Wilmington, North Carolina
SUNDAY MORNING WORSHIP HOUR   (Baptist)

Winston-Salem-Greensboro, North Carolina
CHURCH SERVICE   (Baptist and Presbyterian)

Youngstown, Ohio
SUNDAY SERVICE FROM CALVARY TEMPLE

Inspirational Programs

Abilene, Texas
DEVOTIONS   This series of sermons includes music, pictures, and slides. It is administered through the Ministerial Alliance, which assigns time to member and non-member churches. Sunday, early afternoon, 30 minutes, and Monday-Friday early mornings, five minutes; live; two cameras; 30 minutes rehearsal.

Altoona, Pennsylvania
LIFE OF TRIUMPH   Following a brief musical segment, the pastor of the Altoona Bible Church gives a 20–25 minute sermon. Produced by the station in cooperation with the church. Sunday afternoon; 30 minutes; film; one camera; one hour rehearsal; six hours preparation by station; six hours preparation by participants.

Anchorage, Alaska
PENTECOSTAL CHURCH   Each Saturday a member of the Pentecostal Church delivers a sermon. Produced by station personnel with

the church. Saturday afternoon; 30 minutes; live; one camera; one hour preparation by station.

Anchorage, Alaska
First Assembly of God   This program presents a sermon by a member of the First Assembly of God church. Jointly produced by the station and the church. Sunday afternoon; 30 minutes; tape; studio origination; one camera.

Anchorage, Alaska
Abbott Loop Community Chapel   This program consists of a sermon delivered by a member of the Abbott Loop Community Chapel. Produced by the station with the cooperation with the participating speaker. Sunday afternoon; 30 minutes; live; one camera; one hour preparation by station personnel.

The programs described above are typical of the following. Unless otherwise indicated, programs are offered on Sunday with similar preparation times and use of studio facilities.

Ardmore, Oklahoma
Hamlet Baptist Church   Hymns and a sermon; Saturday morning.

Ardmore, Oklahoma
Christ for the World   Denominational; 15 minutes of choral music and a sermon.

Billings, Montana
Word of Life   Religious songs and a short sermon presented by the Church of God.

Chattanooga, Tennessee
Mull's Singing Convention   Songs by professional and church singing groups; Saturday afternoon.

Chicago, Illinois
CHICAGOLAND'S FAITH   Hymns, interviews, and sermons; ecumenical.

Cincinnati, Ohio
PRAISE HOUR   Sermon and hymns presented by the Council of Churches.

Cincinnati, Ohio
ASBURY HYMN TIME   Gospel singing and a sermon; Saturday morning.

Columbus, Mississippi
VOICE OF TRUTH HOUR   Sermon by Baptist ministers.

Dayton, Ohio
CHURCH BY THE SIDE OF THE ROAD   Sermon produced with the area Church Federation; monthly.

Daytona Beach-Orlando, Florida
TV TABERNACLE   Prayer, music and sermon.

Decatur, Illinois
MEDITATIONS   Sermons by ministers chosen by the Interfaith Committee of the Association of Commerce; Monday-Friday afternoons.

Denver, Colorado
CHURCH OF CHRIST   Sermon with choir background.

Detroit, Michigan
CHURCH AT THE CROSSROADS   Protestant choir selections and sermon. Similar Catholic and Jewish programs are presented.

Detroit, Michigan
CRUSADE FOR CHRIST   Interdenominational religious instruction and hymns; Saturday morning.

Dothan, Alabama
BAPTIST MESSAGE   Sermon, music and announcements; Friday afternoon.

Fargo-Grand Forks, North Dakota
THE KING'S MESSENGERS   Interdenominational sermon and choir singing.

Greensboro, North Carolina
SUNDAY DEVOTIONS   Music by choir and soloist, and sermon by a minister selected by the Ministers' Fellowship.

Greenville, North Carolina
LESSON FOR LIVING   (INTERNATIONAL SUNDAY SCHOOL) Sermon.

Huntsville, Alabama
CENTRAL CHURCH OF CHRIST   Sermon, utilizing rear-screen projection and superimposed slides.

Indianapolis, Indiana
CADLE CHAPEL   Music, prayers and a sermon.

Jackson, Mississippi
REVEREND DUHS.   Readings from the Scriptures and a sermon.

Jacksonville, Florida
KEN KNIGHT SHOW   Negro singers and choral groups, followed by a short sermon.

Jonesboro, Arkansas
GOSPEL OF CHRIST   Sermon and a choir.

Laredo, Texas
CHRISTIAN UNION INSTITUTE   Sermon, hymn singing, and panel discussion; Tuesday evening.

Lexington, Kentucky
PATHWAYS TO GOD   Sermon and hymns by Central Church of God.

Los Angeles, California
MY FAVORITE SERMON   A minister chosen by the Council of Churches presents his best sermon. Includes hymns and religious art, a biography of the minister, and history of his church.

Louisville, Kentucky
SING YE, PRAISE YE   Liturgical music, hymns and a short sermon; ecumenical.

Louisville, Kentucky
SONGS OF FAITH   Music, poetry, singing, prayers and a sermonette; ecumenical.

Mankato, Minnesota
I BELIEVE IN MIRACLES   Religious music and a Baptist inspirational message; Tuesday night.

Miami, Florida
PROTESTANT WORSHIP HOUR   Prayers, Scripture and sermon presented by the local Council of Churches.

Minneapolis-St. Paul, Minnesota
SOUL'S HARBOR   Religious music, choral singing, talks and a sermon.

Missoula, Montana
THE HOUR OF INSPIRATION   Choir and soloists sing religious songs, followed by a sermon and benediction; Saturday evening.

Mobile, Alabama
FEDERATION OF CHURCHES   The Federation of Churches of Mobile present prayers, a sermon and choir songs.

Nashville, Tennessee
COMMUNITY WORSHIP   Music and a talk by a Negro preacher and choir. Tennessee A&I University cooperates in production.

Nashville, Tennessee
LITTLE COUNTRY CHURCH   Gospel music, song and religious readings.

New Born, North Carolina
ORGAN REFLECTION   Organ music supplemented by poetry readings, lighting effects and montages of art works and religious objects.

Norfolk, Virginia
HOUSE OF WORSHIP   Minister and choir, or a panel discussion; ecumenical.

Oak Hill, West Virginia
CHURCH HOME HOUR   A brief sermon, Scripture reading and music; Tuesday evening.

Oklahoma City, Oklahoma
POETRY IN PERSPECTIVE   Religious and secular poems expressed in jazz and interpretive dance.

Port Arthur, Texas
VICTORY ASSEMBLY OF GOD   A short sermon and a choir.

Raleigh, North Carolina
CIRCUIT RIDER   Methodist prayers, music, offering and sermon; commercially sponsored.

Richmond, Virginia
MONUMENT HEIGHTS BAPTIST CHURCH   Choir and a preacher.

Richmond, Virginia
GROVE AVENUE BAPTIST   Preacher and a choir.

Rockford, Illinois
QUEST FOR LIFE   Music, a choir, prayer and discussion.

St. Louis, Missouri
FAITH OF OUR FATHERS   Jewish sermon and music.

St. Louis, Missouri
THE PROTESTANT HOUR   A sermon, choir service and music response.

St. Petersburg-Tampa, Florida
CHURCH SERVICE   Sermon and choir; ecumenical.

Salina, Kansas
SUNDAY SERVICE   Sermon with choir background, produced in association with the Village Missionary Church.

Salt Lake City, Utah
A TIME TO WORSHIP   Sermonette and choir music presented by Salt Lake Council of Churches and local Ministerial Association.

Salt Lake City, Utah
MORMON TABERNACLE CHOIR: MUSIC AND THE SPOKEN WORD   Sermon and musical selections by the famous choir.

San Diego, California
LET THERE BE LIGHT   Religious songs and a sermon; ecumenical.

San Juan, Puerto Rico
CANA EN SU HOGAR   Catholic sermon.

Shreveport, Louisiana
HALLELUJAH TRAIN   Gospel music and a short talk.

Shreveport, Louisiana
THE LIVING WAY   A sermon and singing.

Spokane, Washington
VOICE OF THE CHURCH   Sermon and choir interludes.

Tupelo, Mississippi
THE METHODIST HOUR   Sermon and discussion; Wednesday afternoon.

Wausau, Wisconsin
HOUR OF DELIVERANCE   Sermon.

Weslaco, Texas
YOUR TV PASTOR   Variety show, featuring singing groups and guest ministers; ecumenical.

Weston, West Virginia
MESSAGE OF LIGHT   Hymns, prayers and a short sermon; Saturday.

Briefer Inspirational Programs

Anchorage, Alaska
PASTOR'S STUDY   Ecumenical sermon; Sunday afternoon.

Atlanta, Georgia
CHOIR OF THE WEEK   Hymns and other religious music; ecumenical; Sunday morning.

Austin, Texas
CHRISTIANITY TODAY   Discussion of religious questions, and choir or soloists; Sunday morning.

Bluefield, West Virginia
SPIRITUAL TIME   Negro spirituals; Sunday morning.

Boston, Massachusetts
WE BELIEVE   Brief sermon; ecumenical; Monday-Friday morning.

Charlotte, North Carolina
GOSPEL TRAIN   Gospel music; Sunday morning.

Chicago, Illinois
GREAT HYMNS OF ALL FAITHS   Hymns of the major faiths by soloists or chorus, with organ music as background; Sunday morning.

Cincinnati, Ohio
NOEL SONGS   Gospel singing; Sunday morning.

Columbia, South Carolina
THE LIVING WORD   Short meditative messages; ecumenical; Monday-Friday morning.

Columbus, Mississippi
YOU SHALL KNOW THE TRUTH   Short sermons by the First Christian Church; Thursday evening.

Columbus, Mississippi
THE WAY OF LIFE   Sermon by the Church of Christ; Sunday evening.

Columbus, Mississippi
BACK TO THE BIBLE   Sign-language sermons for the deaf by the Immanuel Baptist Church; Thursday evening.

Columbus, Mississippi
In His Steps   Short Methodist sermonette, with an occasional choral group or soloist; Monday evening.

Dallas, Texas
Young Dallas Sings   Choral music; ecumenical; Sunday morning.

Dallas, Texas
The Baptist Voice   Sermon and choir; Sunday morning.

Dallas, Texas
The Way of Truth   Sermonette and choir presented by the Churches of Christ; Sunday morning.

Dallas, Texas
Words of Life   Sermonette and choir presented by the Assembly of God churches; Sunday morning.

Dallas, Texas
Rabbi Levi Olan   Short sermon; Sunday morning.

Dothan, Alabama
First Baptist Hour   Sermon and choir music; Sunday afternoon.

Elkhart-South Bend, Indiana
Brighten Your Day   Music, comments, announcements, sermon and interview or reading from the Scriptures by the Calvary Temple Church; Wednesday, Thursday, and Friday morning.

Elkhart-South Bend, Indiana
Christ is The Answer   Interviews, religious news, a sermon and occasional dramatic skits presented by the Calvary Temple Church; Sunday afternoon.

Florence, South Carolina
HYMNS FROM THE HILLS   Music and hymns presented in a rural setting; Sunday morning.

Fort Wayne, Indiana
THE BIBLE TODAY   Choral music, solos and a short message by the Assembly of God church; Sunday afternoon.

Great Falls, Montana
THE CHOIRS   Religious music by choirs; ecumenical; Sunday.

Greensboro, North Carolina
MORNING DEVOTIONS   Sermons and choir music; ecumenical; Monday-Friday.

Greenwood, Mississippi
MID-DAY DEVOTIONAL   Noon-time inspirational message based on a reading from Scripture; Monday-Friday.

Houston, Texas
YOUR AREA CHURCHES   Varying format of religious music; ecumenical; Sunday morning.

Jackson, Mississippi
MID-DAY DEVOTIONAL   Sermon; ecumenical; Monday-Friday.

Jackson, Mississippi
VOICE OF GOODWILL   Group singing and a sermon; Sunday morning.

Johnson City, Tennessee
MELODY TIME   Gospel singing; Thursday night.

Knoxville, Tennessee
MULL'S SINGING CONVENTION   Gospel singing; Sunday morning.

Lafayette, Louisiana
The Rosary   Prayers; daily.

Laredo, Texas
Spiritual Refreshment   Methodist sermon, discussion and hymn singing; Tuesday afternoon.

Laredo, Texas
Laredo Ministerial Association   Sermon and hymn singing; Thursday afternoon.

Laurel-Hattiesburg, Mississippi
The Pastor's Corner   Sermon presented by the local Ministerial Association; daily; afternoon.

Laurel-Hattiesburg, Mississippi
The Way of Life   Sermon presented by the Central Baptist Church; Saturday morning.

Lincoln-Grand Island, Nebraska
Choir Loft   Inspirational music and song by local choirs; Sunday afternoon.

Memphis, Tennessee
Above the Clouds   Devotional program of music and voice presented by the Memphis Union Mission; Monday-Friday morning.

Meridian, Mississippi
Faith for Everyday Living   Protestant sermon with music by pianist or accordianist; Monday-Friday.

Miami, Florida
Give Us This Day   Daily sign-on sermon; ecumenical.

Missoula, Montana
TED SCOTT SHOW   Organ music and a short sermon or prayer; Friday evening.

Mobile, Alabama
RELIGION IN YOUR LIFE   Sermon; Sunday morning.

Monroe-West Monroe, Louisiana
FOR TIMES LIKE THESE   Short sermon, mood music, vocal selections by a choral group, and dramatic enactment of religious experiences presented by the First Baptist Church; Sunday afternoon.

Nashville, Tennessee
HEAVEN'S JUBILEE   Hymns and Gospel singing; Sunday.

Nashville, Tennessee
OLD TIME SINGING CONVENTION   Gospel music interspersed with thoughts for the day; Monday-Friday.

Norfolk, Virginia
LIFT UP MINE EYES   Sermonette or discussion; ecumenical; Monday-Friday.

Oklahoma City, Oklahoma
MORNING DEVOTIONS   Short devotional message; ecumenical; Monday-Friday.

Paducah, Kentucky
THE PASTOR SPEAKS   Religious messages by members of the local Ministerial Association; Monday-Friday; noon.

Port Arthur, Texas
STREAMS OF FAITH   Short inspirational sermon; Sunday morning.

Raleigh, North Carolina
Gospel Caravan   Spirituals and gospel singing; partially sponsored; Sunday morning.

Raleigh, North Carolina
The Harvesters   Hymns and gospel songs; Saturday night.

Richmond, Virginia
Guidepost to Happiness   Sermon and organ music; Sunday morning.

Rockford, Illinois
Sermon for a Sunday   Sermon by members of the Rockford Ministerial Associations; Sunday morning.

St. Louis, Missouri
Message of The Rabbi   Sermon by members of the Rabbinical Association; Sunday morning.

St. Paul-Minneapolis, Minnesota
Hymn Time   Hymns and sacred songs with a background of illustrations and religious scenes; Sunday morning.

San Diego, California
Youth for Christ   Religious songs and brief inspirational messages; Sunday morning.

Santa Barbara, California
Inspiration   Inspirational message and choral music; Sunday afternoon.

Seattle, Washington
Note of Faith   An ecumenical sign-off and sign-on series of recorded religious music and films showing the wonders of nature; twice daily.

Selma, Alabama
GOSPEL TIME IN DIXIE   Religious musical performance; Thursday evening.

Shreveport, Louisiana
YOUR PASTOR   Sermonette and prayer; ecumenical; Monday-Friday morning.

Springfield, Massachusetts
LIFT UP YOUR VOICES   Once-monthly program of songs by choirs from local Negro churches.

Steubenville, Ohio-Wheeling, West Virginia
THE GREATEST OF THESE   Dramatic scenes, silhouette action, film, slides and pictures portray religious themes; Catholic; Sunday afternoon.

Tupelo, Mississippi
SERMONETTE   Sermon by members of the Tupelo Ministerial Association; weekday afternoons.

Yuma, Arizona
VOICE OF CALVARY   Talk by a pastor and choral music; Saturday afternoon.

Meditations

The following are meditations which begin and end the telecasting day (sign-on and sign-off):

Atlanta, Georgia
EVENING REFLECTIONS   Ecumenical sermon.

Bangor, Maine
OPEN DOOR   Brief ecumenical sermon by a local minister.

Birmingham, Alabama
DAILY DEVOTIONAL   Short inspirational messages seen at various times during the day as well as at sign-on and sign-off.

Champaign, Illinois
INSPIRATIONAL TIME   Inspirational thoughts by local ministers at sign-on.

Chicago, Illinois
FIVE MINUTES TO LIVE BY   Short sermonettes delivered by clergymen of the major faiths.

Chico, California
SIGN OUT   Inspirational messages delivered by local ministers.

Cincinnati, Ohio
SIGN-ON AND SIGN-OFF   Methodist inspirational messages.

Cincinnati, Ohio
FIVE MINUTES TO LIVE BY   Representatives of the three major faiths rotate in presenting an inspirational message at sign-on.

Cleveland, Ohio
MEDITATION   Inspirational messages delivered by clergymen of the major faiths.

Cleveland, Ohio
CREDO   Sermons delivered by clergymen of the major faiths.

Columbia, South Carolina
IN HIS SERVICE   Sign-on sermon by local clergymen.

Columbus, Ohio
FIVE MINUTES TO LIVE BY   Short Protestant inspirational messages.

Corpus Christi, Texas
CHURCH OF CHRIST   Church of Christ sermon.

Dallas, Texas
MORNING AND EVENING DEVOTIONS   Devotional messages and prayer delivered by clergymen of the major faiths.

Dayton, Ohio
INSPIRATION   Ecumenical inspirational messages.

Denver, Colorado
MEDITATIONS   Baptist sermon.

Detroit, Michigan
CONSIDER THIS   Ecumenical sign-off sermon.

El Paso, Texas
MORNING AND EVENING DEVOTIONALS   Sign-on and sign-off sermons by members of the local Ministerial Alliance.

Fresno, California
INSPIRATION   Ecumenical devotional messages.

Indianapolis, Indiana
FIVE MINUTES TO LIVE BY   Inspirational messages by members of the Indianapolis Church Federation.

Jackson, Mississippi
LAYMEN'S PRAYER   Prayers delivered by members of the Ministerial Alliance.

Jacksonville, Florida
PASTOR'S STUDY   Brief inspirational messages given by members of the Ministerial Alliance.

Jacksonville, Florida
LIVING WORDS   Brief devotional messages by local ministers.

Lansing, Michigan
THOUGHT FOR THE DAY   Musical introduction and a sermon by members of the Council of Churches.

Lexington, Kentucky
TAKE FIVE   Local clergymen from the Council of Churches and Ministerial Association alternate in delivering an inspirational message.

Lexington, Kentucky
RELIGIOUS VIGNETTE   Message from the Bible read by the Bishop of the Episcopal Diocese of Central Valley.

Memphis, Tennessee
TV CHAPEL   Representatives of the three major faiths rotate in presenting sermons.

Miama, Florida
INSPIRATIONAL MESSAGES   Short inspirational messages delivered by clergymen of the major faiths.

Milwaukee, Wisconsin
TV CHAPEL   Short prayers, inspirational messages, and passages from the Bible presented by local clergymen.

Minneapolis, Minnesota
DIRECTION   Short talks of an inspirational nature.

Minneapolis, Minnesota
LIVE TODAY   Inspirational messages.

Minneapolis-St. Paul, Minnesota
POWER FOR TOMORROW   Short sermonette delivered by a local clergyman.

Mobile, Alabama
PASTOR'S STUDY   Short talks by members of the Federation of Churches of Mobile.

Monroe-West Monroe, Louisiana
PASTOR'S STUDY   Inspirational message and prayer given by a local clergyman.

Montgomery, Alabama
PASTOR'S STUDY   Sermon by members of the Montgomery Ministerial Association.

Montgomery, Alabama
THOUGHT FOR TODAY   Brief inspirational messages by members of the local Ministerial Association.

Nashville, Tennessee
FIVE GOLDEN MINUTES   Sermonette and music.

New York, New York
GIVE US THIS DAY   Clergymen of the three major faiths present thoughts for the day.

New York, New York
REFLECTIONS   Sermons, dramatic readings, music and poetry at sign-off.

Oklahoma City, Oklahoma
REFLECTIONS   Varying format, including reading from the Scriptures, poetry, play or a sermon, slides and music.

Omaha, Nebraska
AT DAY'S END   Laymen explain their reasons for believing in God.

Onondaga, Michigan
PATHWAYS TO FAITH   Sermons delivered by members of the Ministerial Association.

Phoenix, Arizona
MEDITATION   Short inspirational message.

Portland, Oregon
TIME FOR MEDITATION   Music, a short sermon and a prayer by the Greater Portland Council of Churches.

Rochester, New York
PASTORAL CALL   Inspirational messages by local clergymen.

Rochester, New York
DEVOTIONS   A local clergyman delivers a short inspirational sermon at sign-on and sign-off.

Rockford, Illinois
THOUGHT FOR TODAY   Ministers who rotate weekly present short inspirational messages.

Rock Island, Illinois
WE BEGIN THIS DAY   Brief inspirational messages.

Salt Lake City, Utah
BLESSINGS OF A NEW DAY—DAY'S END PRAYER   Inspirational messages by representatives of the various faiths, combined with film and slides of the churches.

Salt Lake City, Utah
THOUGHT FOR THE DAY   Scriptual readings by local clergymen.

Santa Barbara, California
INSPIRATIONAL MESSAGE Filmed inspirational messages by churches in the local area, seen on a rotating basis.

Seattle, Washington
THOUGHT FOR THE DAY Inspirational message by representatives of the three major faiths.

Shreveport, Louisiana
VESPERS Talk by a local clergyman using a filmed hymn as background.

Sioux Falls, South Dakota
THOUGHT FOR TODAY Sermon based on a Biblical thought delivered by two local pastors.

Tulsa, Oklahoma
LIGHT OF LIFE Sermon delivered by a minister selected by the local Council of Churches.

Washington, D. C.
TODAY IN YOUR LIFE Talks by representatives of the three major faiths.

Wheeling, West Virginia
WINDOW TOWARD GOD—LET THERE BE LIGHT Sermons by a Protestant minister and a Catholic priest.

Wilmington, North Carolina
THESE THINGS WE SHARE Brief inspirational message by a local minister.

Winston-Salem-Greensboro, North Carolina
TODAY'S PRAYER Bible reading, prayer and thought for the day, by members of the Forsyth Ministers' Fellowship.

Youngstown, Ohio
MORNING MEDITATION   A local minister and members of his family present a brief sermon and two hymns.

The following are meditations and devotional messages presented at other times of the day:

Bluefield, West Virginia
THOUGHT FOR TODAY   Short sermons by the Bluefield Ministers' Association, presented during the *Today* show.

Florence, South Carolina
MEDITATION   A pastor in an informal setting delivers a short inspirational message and prayer; Monday-Friday afternoon.

Fort Myers, Florida
THE LATEST WORD   Brief inspirational messages by a local minister; Friday evening.

Idaho Falls, Idaho
TIME FOR MEDITATION   Prayer or sermon offered by members of the Idaho Falls Ministerial Association; Sunday morning.

Mobile, Alabama
COFFEE WITH THE PARSON   Baptist inspirational message; weekday mornings.

Raleigh, North Carolina
MINUTE FOR MEDITATION   Short inspirational messages offered on a rotating basis by clergymen of many denominations; evenings, at the start of network programming.

Richmond, Virginia
DR. THEO ADAMS-INSPIRATIONALS   Inspirational talks inserted at various times in the broadcast schedule.

Roanoke, Virginia
PRAYER FOR GUIDANCE   Non-sectarian prayers; three times a day, weekdays.

Roswell, New Mexico
WORDS AND MUSIC   Inspirational poems and devotionals with live organ music; Saturday afternoon.

Savannah, Georgia
DAILY DEVOTION   Sermon by ministers who appear on a rotating basis. A sign-language interpreter presents the sermon for the deaf on Fridays; Monday-Friday afternoons.

South Bend, Indiana
DAILY MEDITATIONS   Sermons by ministers of the local Council of Churches; Monday-Friday afternoons.

". . . Unless we solicit decisions, we are failing the most awe-inspiring idea that ever engaged the mind of man—the redemptive idea, the changed-man philosophy. . . . No responsible broadcaster would schedule a series of commercials not calculated to elicit decisions, decisions to buy certain products or services, decisions to take advantage of certain opportunities. And any astute broadcaster knows that unless decisions are made in response to his persuasion, he isn't going to be in the persuading business very long."

—Theodore M. Lott
The Beam, August, 1965.

IV

GUIDELINES FOR THE RELIGIOUS PROGRAM PLANNER

An Approach

At the heart of any programming approach must lie some sense of the conditions of audience reception in the home. It is understood, of course, that the television medium is impersonal in the larger sense. Yet it may be argued that TV is also both intimate and highly personal, for the fact that great numbers of human beings experience an identical communication at the same time need not imply that all viewers undergo identical perceptual experiences. Research evidence supports what is by now obvious— that a massed group of individuals is *not* the same thing as a mass audience, particularly if it is assumed that such an audience is somehow responding in a universal and homogenized way.

Response to television (indeed to all of the so-called mass media) is far from uniform and immediate. Critic John Crosby once argued that the more important the values and beliefs people hold are to them, the less likely the media are to sway them. In fact, his intuitive judgement is supported by research which indicates that television's power lies in its capacity to reinforce selectively rather than to convert people's beliefs and attitudes. The religious program planner must, therefore, recognize that his efforts are more likely to succeed if he will set out to discover and raise the intensity of already existing motivations rather than attempt to change values and attitudes over any short period of time.

It is necessary to begin with the assumption that the viewer is lightly engaged—that he is at home, shielded from the necessities of social amenity, privately ensconced amidst the smaller reality of family and in command of the medium which, as conventional wisdom would have it, was supposed to be in command of him. It is the viewer who is shaping the medium, not the opposite. It is he who is *selecting*, both physically (by simply switching the set on and off) and psychologically (by accepting or rejecting what he sees, hears and chooses to believe) what will emerge from his home receiver. If, as some studies reveal, the greatest numbers of human beings retain favorable dispositions and attitudes toward faith and the religious experience, then the religious program planner already has a distinct advantage, for he can begin at the outset to raise the intensity of such motivation by dealing with the viewer *as* he is and *where* he is.

If those who plan religious programs will seek that human element which lies at the core of television's greatest attractions to the individuals of the *massed* audience, and if they will trouble to acquire a detailed understanding of the communicative techniques which enhance these elements, they will be well disposed for the task at hand. The planner's outlook must include an appreciation of not merely how to use television techniques to transmit a body of doctrine, but of what can be said with dignity and integrity in the kind of relationship which exists between the viewer and the telecaster. His approach must be based upon a sharpened sense of realism concerning viewer motivation and a heightened appreciation for the telecaster's hard-won professional knowledge of "what works."

Establishing Priorities

The first step in developing successful religious messages for TV is to establish clear priorities in communicative purpose. Once these are set forth, they must be accompanied by some reasonable effort to keep each kind of priority separate and distinct from the others throughout the specific stages of message conceptualization and design.

Each of the following priorities (adapted from a report produced at a recent conference on Religious Television conducted in England) suggests a broad, separate range of program conceptualizations. These ideas for program types and formats will in turn lead to specific planning (definition of intended audience; choice of day and time for presentation; length and frequency of messages). Once these are determined, the groundwork is laid for the final stages of message design and execution: production planning (involving personnel and budget); studio and facilities utilization (involving basic production method, scenery and settings, technical needs, graphics and still photographs); scripting; talent selection and rehearsal.

The first of the broader purposes which can be assigned to religious television is *to awaken and develop a sense of the depth and mystery of life and of man's personal and corporate responsibilities in the contemporary world.* Assigning this priority will enable the religious program planner to limit his considerations to those programs and messages which relate to man's search for meaning through his arts and cultural expressions. The priority suggests appeal to the viewer primarily through his aesthetic sensibilities. The kinds of programs or shorter messages to be developed in service of this purpose are varied: musical; dramatic; narrative programs devoted to formally "religious art" or expression of the religious spirit in all art; oral interpretation of prose and of poetry; the dance; works of cinematic art; and specialized documentary programs—either with art as a subject or as examples of the documentary art in themselves.

To be sure, the conceptualizations need not result in creation of what is termed "art-product." Programs serving this priority may be cast in conventional discussion or interview program formats. It can be as stimulating and moving, for example, to hear a famous poet or dramatist discuss his work as to see and hear the work performed. A discussion by playwrights or painters on the contemporary search for spiritual meaning in their respective crafts may be as valuable as seeing the examples of the art, and the combination of approaches (a scene from a drama followed by a discussion of the moral dilemmas it poses; the performance of religious music coupled with spoken observations about the composer's expressive intentions) has been usefully and imaginatively employed in a variety of national and local religious programs.

Planning this kind of TV communication, however, will introduce specific challenges. As he contemplates artistic presentations of larger scope, the planner must naturally consider the suitability of available talent, costs of production and the inevitable question of the kind of audience his efforts will attract. The more obscure and remote the subject material (hence the narrower and more specialized the interests of the audience), the less inclined the telecaster will be to assign high-priority air-time to its treatment, let alone the professional talents of his staff. If he wishes to maximize the impact of his work, the planner must seek out the potentially wider appeals within the subject material itself and be prepared to suggest possibilities for their development to the telecaster. A hard-hitting documentary, a provocative drama or an intense discussion of controversial developments in a given art form need not be more appealing than a quiet examination of church architecture in a given community, if the latter can be produced with skill and imagination. One need only consider the witty series of visual essays produced by Andrew Rooney for CBS-TV on such prosaic subjects as chairs, doors and bridges. The local religious programmer may not hope to duplicate the unique combination of filmic artistry, Rooney's intelligent writing and Harry Reasoner's wry and disarming commentary, but he must be able to present to the telecaster the impact potentialities of his subject which might be developed by the professional staff of the local station.

It must be assumed at the outset that the programs conceived in this area of service will usually be relatively expensive to produce well; they will probably require a high degree of professionalism in production; and, above all, they will require performing talent. All of this implies a more intense involvement and effort upon the part of the station production staff.

A second major purpose of religious television is *to present the historical foundations of the religious experience as well as the continuing presence of man's religious experience and institutions in the world today.* By establishing this priority, the programmer may once again place at least some flexible limitations upon his development of types of programs and messages. Obviously, any kind of communication may answer such broad purpose, but it is useful to focus attention in this area upon certain basic designs: formal instructional or educational programs, religious information programs and all transmissions of religious worship and inspirational activities. Again, the number of specific approaches which can be taken is great, although a number of conventional and traditional formats are already established. Because a program is formally designated as "instructional" or "educational," however, does not limit the imagination to what is already being done. There is an infinite number of creative possibilities, in all stages of conception and execution, which can make such traditional approaches to life. The "lecture with visuals" approach to instruction may be valuable in some cases, but there are many ways in which instruction can be made more challenging and compelling. Similarly, informational programming need not be routinely conceived in terms of an announcer reading bulletins from the local churches.

The religious programmer will face his greatest challenge, however, in the presentation of formal religious services and inspirational and meditational messages. Since transmission of formal services places strict limitations upon the role which television as a medium can play in building viewer interest, there are a num-

ber of questions the religious programmer might ask of himself
and the institution he serves. What is the value, for example, of
transmitting a weekly church service at all? Beyond the necessary
service to shut-ins and others who cannot attend church, might
the time and energy expended be put to better use? What value
does a televised formal religious service have? Is there evidence
that those who could, but do not, attend church services watch
them on TV at home? Would the time be better devoted to programs of an inspirational nature which can influence already-
existing favorable attitudes toward religion—thereby increasing
regular church attendance? Above all, are the religious programmer and the telecaster doing all they can to assure that the inspirational programs themselves are not simply repetitious, unimag-
inatively presented and routine?

The third broad purpose of religious television is *to reflect the
continuing dialogue between the church and the world*. One
might speculate that no priority for religious television deserves
greater effort and attention on the part of both program planner
and telecaster, for television has evolved new and dramatic modes
of transmission of the information and experience which underlie
our social understanding. If the medium can serve well both the
aesthetic and spiritual needs of men and society, it is at least ar-
guable that it is functioning at its best when its efforts are devoted to presentation of the actualities of the daily social experience. The burgeoning of news and public affairs programming in
the past decade attest to the medium's involvement in recording
our social conflicts and confrontations. This thrust demands that
the religious program planner give greater attention to engaging
the growing audience for news and information.

In assigning this priority to religious television still another
group of program conceptions is suggested. Here is where the development of discussion and debate programs, documentary and
semi-documentary forms devoted to current controversies, talk and
interview programs which focus upon social issues and dilemmas
—all as related to the religious outlook and the deeper spiritual
needs of society—should be undertaken. The range of possibilities is wide, but all programs and messages conceived in service

of this goal should focus upon the immediacies and realities of daily life in our national experience. And it is here that the opportunities for attracting increased audiences to religious broadcasting are greatest. The vast majority of human beings are and always have been most interested in the social, political and moral issues which will affect them most—which will have greatest relevance to their own position in the social structure—and to the changes in society which will have most direct influence upon them. The religious programmer would do well to consider this concern as he begins to relate his message to society.

It should be made clear that no program conceptualizations or resulting formats must necessarily reflect a single purpose in religious television. Assigning priorities is useful because it may help to bring into focus the more specific problems relating to proper use of the medium. It will, first of all, assist the planner in defining his intended audience. And as he makes certain decisions about the kind, and number, of people he is preparing his message for, he can also begin to work more realistically with the telecaster on such matters as time of day and frequency of scheduling. He can begin to bring into balance the nature of the intended audience with the real prospects of gaining the viewer's time and attention. He will be better prepared to deal with the principle that degree of attention is directly proportional to program interest and attractiveness. It is not enough for him to decide that a certain kind of content could attract greater attention if placed at a better time within the program schedule. Unless his messages have certain basic audience appeals, they will not increase attention either quantitatively (size of audience) or qualitatively (impact upon the viewer). It is useful, therefore, to consider next more specific ways in which the religious program specialist can make his efforts more attractive to audiences.

Seeking Professional Quality

The survey reported in this volume requested that respondents offer some of their own professional observations and suggestions for improving the quality of religious programs. Their responses would, if elaborated upon, constitute an entire textbook in the communicative arts of television. The need for better scripts, more imaginative planning and more entertaining production was cited again and again. A frequently-named shortcoming was the failure of speakers to distinguish between the congregation in the church and the audience in the home. A variety of suggestions covering the specific problems of attaining more interesting production, choice of subject and approach and the need to adopt a "professional attitude" were offered. In the main, the suggestions for current programs tend to focus upon the general need to make religious communication in television more exciting and compelling. The commentary prompts some deeper analysis here.

First, programming will improve when producing agencies recognize the need for those audience appeals which have been clearly established in other forms of TV programming and attempt to integrate them with taste and integrity into their own efforts. Unquestionably, the most vital of these appeals are *conflict* and *humor*. Few truly great programs or program series in the history of public communication have succeeded in attracting and holding audiences, large or small, without the dramatic appeals of either conflict or humor, or some combination of both.

In *The Act of Creation*, Arthur Koestler[1] examines a number of theories and observations on the way in which people respond to experience and he has recast them brilliantly into an inclusive theory which explains not only man's tragic and comic senses, but his intellectual power. Man tends to develop patterns or habits of attitude and response as he comes to know the world around him. These Koestler calls "matrices" of experience and he observes that when a matrix of human mental activity (a "set" way of looking at new things within a psychological framework of accustomed patterns of response, value, attitude and thought) is suddenly confronted with an unexpected set of circumstances or situations, the two matrices of thought must be reconciled. Koestler writes that the human mind must respond in a process called "bisociation" and the result is either *confrontation* (which leads him,

[1] Arthur Koestler, *The Act of Creation* (New York, Dell, 1967), p. 35 et seq.

figuratively, to cry); *collision* (which leads him to laugh); or *fusion* (which leads him to wonder, inquire and investigate).

Whether or not the theory accounts for all of human tears and laughter, it is useful in that it explains man's capacity to sense the antic as well as the tragic. It also demonstrates that the capacities to laugh, cry and think are inseparable elements within the human mind. The wholly successful communication, it may be said, is one which can involve all stages of this mental activity—moving man to wonder and inquire through the stimulation of other fundamental responses.

Such broad theory can be given application in efforts to make religious communication on TV more effective. The oldest dramaturgical laws of "man-against-man, man-against-nature, man-against-himself," for example, hold relevance in any form of communication. The presentation of opposing forces and the dramatic "pull" of an unknown outcome command the attention of almost all human beings, whether they be framed in terms of a football game or a controversial discussion of religious beliefs. The confrontation of human wills, whether at the subtler level of sharp intellectual debate or the violent exertions of two boxers, is an essential element underlying audience attention and the religious programmer is obliged to provide some element of this appeal if he wishes to engage greater numbers of his audience. Further, the history of television programming reveals that the size of the audience will bear a direct relationship to the simplicity and directness of the confrontation which is posed.

It is fruitless to engage in dispute over whether exploitation of this human need is "harmful" in its effects. If such argument were taken seriously, man's art, his spiritual aspiration and his expressions of concern over the destiny of his social order would be nonexistent. Argument in this matter is justified only when the program producer fails to distinguish between *violence* and *conflict* in human action.

Whatever format he chooses, the programmer in the religious field is obliged to seek elements within his content which juxtapose the inherently opposing forces and he must then so build his presentation that these may heighten the viewer's involvement at once. All great men of the pulpit have a way of framing "the dramatic question" at the outset of a sermon—the habit of posing a spiritual or moral confrontation in order to involve and gain the attention of the congregation and, subsequently, to relate their own needs to the dilemmas which are posed.

Introduction of this element, therefore, does not imply the selection of dramatic formats alone. Any talk, discussion or interview program can hold elements of latent confrontation. The viewer is more attentive when he observes the inward struggle of a person interviewed—when the questioning is, within the bounds of good taste, sharp and decisive. A discussion program in which no differences of opinion are in evidence will entice few to attend and the more these differences can be heightened and focused by an intelligent moderator, the more attention will be gained.

Categorically, the religious programmer should seek every means by which to identify and make clear the potential confrontations of forces which exist in his subject. If none are to be discovered, then he should look for, and exploit if possible the second major appeal, humor.

The appeal of the comic is universal; to deny the introduction of such an appeal into the spiritual message would be to shut off one significant road to wider audience response. Hence the religious programmer must also seek to integrate light and humorous elements into his message where appropriate. Again, such material may be embraced within a variety of formats, ranging from comedy-dramas to talks which feature a speaker with wit and a telling humorous style—that great capacity to sense the potential sources of humor in situations.

It is important to remember that no form of public communication can generate any large-scale audience involvement and attention if the message does not incorporate one of the two major appeals to the human spirit into its presentation. It is equally important for all who are engaged in religious programming to understand that the inclusion of these appeals will not limit their capacity to deal with complex intellectual matters. Nor will it limit the potential make-up of their audience. The essentially recreational nature of television cannot be denied. The audience for a football game, a good mystery drama or a great comedy program simply does not divide along the lines of demarcation mapped by conventional pundits writing about the TV audience. The college professor may enjoy a baseball game, while the truck-driver may enjoy a serious discussion presented in a dynamic fashion. This hardly eliminates the need for planners to consider the subtlety with which conflict and comedy may be introduced into programs, but this is a matter of degree rather than substance.

The religious programmer must also look to a number of lesser audience appeals which can and should inform his conceptualization. The elements of "human interest," "participation," and "familiarity" are not to be overlooked, even though they are often related in complex ways to the basic appeals of conflict and comedy. Human beings are captivated and involved, for example, when they see and hear other interesting human beings presented as themselves. Hence the success of the "human interest" program since the *Vox Pop* days of radio. Whether it is the "average" man or the celebrity, the nonprofessional performer who is articulate can exert a dramatic hold over an audience. The viewer enjoys witnessing the human drama in the faces and voices of others with "a story to tell" of how they have met life's conflicts and vagaries.

When this "human interest" appeal can be harnessed in service of spiritual involvement the impact may be great indeed. I have argued elsewhere that the greatest single strength of televised communications is the "talking-face"—*if* those who select those faces and personalities are sensitive to the depth and meaning which lie beneath the surface. It is too easy for program planners to regard this aspect lightly. In their quest for "visualization," they may forget that cinematic and theatrical splendors on the small screen are valueless if there is no real point of human contact and involvement.

The appeal of "familiarity" is also too often overlooked in developing religious programs. Because of the relaxed pattern of

TV message perception in the home, there is some value in attempting wherever possible to include those elements which can reflect and intensify the viewer's comfortable sense of "belonging." This quality may be expressed in the presence of a discussion moderator who is a popular and well-known local figure, or in the established elements in any program format which build a feeling of relaxed receptivity. Over the years every great television performer has had his own special song, theme or mode of instant (often nostalgic) identification which the audience, accustomed to such familiar and "old-shoe" elements, finds instantly familiar and comforting. Beyond these, there are positive aspects of "familiarity" in the performer, in the program format and in the theme and identifying materials which carry appeal in their own right. The religious programmer would do well to seek the development of this appeal wherever possible.

Additionally, the design and plans for religious programming should incorporate, again where possible and appropriate, the appeal of "participation." Such appeal is normally generated in audience "write-in" or "phone-in" programs, but there is also a broader level at which the appeal generates interest. The appearance of a guest or speaker from a viewer's hometown or neighborhood obviously will involve viewers from the area at a higher level, giving them a sense of participation they might not otherwise have. Perhaps the strength of the appeal is best illustrated by the feelings of a viewer whose favorite football team is playing in the big game as contrasted with his watching teams which mean little to him.

Clearly, none of these appeals stands alone in its impact upon the TV viewer. In combination, their presence can assure the planner that he is maximizing the potential for creating interest. Programs and messages which do not in some way involve one or more of these elements will not be interesting, entertaining or worthy of attention. And it must be stressed once more that the search for, and inclusion of, these appeals does not negate or in any way limit the possibilities for creative excellence, a desire to satisfy aesthetic sensibility or intellectual significance. The intentions of the programmer may be serious, subtle and capable of comprehension only by a limited audience of high intellectual attainment or they may easily be comprehended and directed toward an audience which is merely seeking diversion—but at neither extreme will an audience be engaged if no basic appeals are generated.

Some Practical Applications

Titles

One of religious television's most obvious needs is to discover fresh program titles. It is worthwhile to avoid the stock words and phrases which are so readily associated with what critics have called the "Sunday ghetto." Even when considerable care is devoted to quality and interesting content, the casual assignment of a dull and overworked title will work against audience interest from the outset. Such titles as *The Pastors' Study* and *The (Anyfaith) Hour* have been overused to the point where potential viewers have already developed negative attitudes toward the programs they describe. One need only consider the impact of the title of the first program in the *Directions '65* series—"Will The Real Jesus Christ Please Stand Up?"—in order to appreciate the attraction which a provocative and even controversial program title can have for viewers.

It is true that series titles are difficult to change once they are established, but individual titles can be made decidedly more exciting—and emphasized in publicity. If half the inventiveness and imagination devoted to the clever sermon titles posted in front of American churches were applied to naming religious TV programs, a positive gain in viewership might be achieved.

Choosing Performers

Penry Jones of ABC Television in England points out that the experience provided in the great cathedral cannot be duplicated in television and this applies most particularly in the conditions of delivery of the sermon. "Not everyone knows," said Jones, that some of the preachers most admired in their denominations are preachers whom we know we cannot use in television—preachers who are so peripatetic, maybe, that they will wander backwards and forwards and make the viewers seasick. Any preacher worth his salt is capable of castigating his congregation from on high in a pulpit. In TV, however, the situation is reversed. For the viewer, the preacher is a manikin $14\frac{1}{2}$ inches high, and not distorted if he is lucky, and it is ludicrous to expect him to do the same thing as you can in a public meeting or in some churches.

The same observation has often been made in America, most recently by Edward Stanley,[2] who while he was at NBC, noted that the style of the pulpit is not the proper style for effective TV communication and asked for a new intimacy in delivery.

The elements which may introduce added pace and excitement into religious programs are varied, but none is so essential as professional performance. The central personality of the program makes all of the difference and, if the format is talk or discussion, it is obviously the single most vital factor in program success. People have not watched Bishop Sheen in order to be stimulated by glamorous "production numbers" or clever visual effects. Program individuality and uniqueness lie solely within the talents of Bishop Sheen. Another speaker might adopt the same themes and be surrounded by the same production aids and techniques without generating any viewer interest at all. It is the style of the man which subtly informs the elements of dramatic pacing and structure. The late Edward R. Murrow once observed that the best writing is done by people who, in speaking, are "armed with their own convictions," and the success of *See It Now* might well be examined by those who seek to involve an audience in matters of spiritual concern.

Interview and Discussion

The requirements for success in interview and discussion programs are not beyond the reach of local programming agencies. Needed are a skilled, knowledgeable and inquisitive interviewer

2 Edward Stanley, *TV Age* (Aug. 2, 1965), p. 26 et seq.

who respects the expertise and character of the people he is questioning, and an interviewee who has done his homework. Too often, the interviewer prepares his list of questions in advance and then proceeds through them at a uniform rate—as though determined not to listen to the answers at all. At other times, the interviewer will forget that he is not the central personality, and will brow-beat, confuse and otherwise embarrass the interviewee in order to satisfy his own ego. If the interviewer fails to respond to what the interviewee is saying, all hope for a spontaneous and entertaining presentation of information is gone.

The flaws in interview programming, however, do not always rest with the person asking the questions. Preachers, as well as politicians, too often prepare for an interview by trying to guess what the questions will be—in order to avoid answering them! Obviously, the best interviewees are those who make a firm effort to understand the question and then address themselves directly to it. Too many respondents are prepared to say only what they intend to say, regardless of what questions are asked. If they are clever enough, they present only their point of view, and the interviewer's questions are left unanswered.

If both interviewer and interviewee will take the trouble to consider the viewer's interest in gaining solid opinion and information, such programs stand a fair chance for success. This by no means implies that either should suppress his own personality and point of view. An interviewee without firm convictions, informed opinions and his own framework of relevance is of very little interest. If he attempts to suppress these, it is the responsibility of the questioner to dig for them—to spark response by pointed and intelligent queries. It is understood, of course, that he will proceed in good taste and with respect for the integrity of his guest.

The key, however, is that both parties to the discussion *listen* and *respond* to what the other is saying. This rule must apply in those interviews which are purely informative in nature as well as in those whose primary aim is the study of human character. It is interesting, of course, to study the faces and hear the opinions of the great and near-great, and yet both producers and interviewers

—as a result of the heightened interest which working with such people in a studio provides—forget that the home viewer is robbed of that dimension which the living presence of an interesting person adds to a conversation. The result is that "human interest" guests are often allowed to ramble beyond points of interest and conviction. They begin to drift and the professional interviewer (or the producer), for the sake of his guest as well as for the sake of audience involvement, must edit. He must frame, form and constantly adjust emphasis for the sake of pace and point. If it is a filmed interview, the responsibility is largely the producer's; in a live interview it is the host-interviewer who must keep control. Inexperience and lack of skill in editing will inevitably result in a rambling and disassociated conversation.

Brief Inspirational Messages

The value and significance of the briefer program and short announcement is often overlooked by religious program planners. The short "spot" announcement is seldom used at all and the great numbers of brief inspirational or meditational messages now on TV are seldom given the creative attention they deserve. Yet the entire mode of TV communication suggests that these may have considerable influence upon the intensity of existing audience predispositions and attitudes. The wise political campaigner in America has learned that 60-second spot announcements may have greater impact upon the TV audience than full-length political programs and the assignment of campaign budgets has been made accordingly. Some experimentation has been conducted in the use of spots at the national level for the reinforcement of already-existing favorable attitudes toward religion. While there has been some resistance among church spokesmen to the cleverly stylized Stan Freberg "go to church" spots and the "God is Alive" series, they have some value in that the audience apparently pays attention to and enjoys them.

Such brief announcements need not be humorous in nature, although the catchiness of humor has a wide attraction. It is demonstrably true that "most people most of the time" enjoy the brevity and the emotional stimulation of such messages. Since such messages reflect the recreational desires which lead viewers to watch TV in the first place, they will tend to observe and be stimulated by their conciseness and sharpened appeal—an attraction which is becoming more evident to professional observers of the medium. In an apt and insightful analysis of TV commercials, Professor Gerald Weales of the University of Pennsylvania English Department has observed that the best of them tell, in their own way, a full dramatic story in 60 seconds or less: setting a problem, introducing characters, carrying them to a dramatic crisis or "moment of truth" and presenting a clear (usually happy, of course) resolution to the problem, which effects an audience "release."

While some would object to the "marketing" of religion in this way, it is less than fair to condemn a *technique* which is successful and undoubtedly influential simply because it is also employed to elicit decisions to buy products and services. Brevity, the dramatic impact of conflict and resolution, genuinely creative graphic and cinematic technique, humor, taut and exciting structure—these are the vital elements of all successful art and communication, irrespective of the purpose served. St. Francis Productions has distributed several series of 20-, 30- and 60-second messages of inspiration, best described as "soft sell telespots."

It would be useful if considerably more attention were also devoted to the brief inspirational programs. While it is undoubtedly of value for local churches to participate in presentations of "thoughts for the day" and innumerable sign-on and sign-off "meditations," many of these seem to be perfunctory and routine in both conception and execution. There is as yet too little experiment in the creation of a moving and compelling series of visual images to accompany short verbal messages. Admittedly, such effort requires extra planning (and will increase budgets), yet the added care in preparation could produce an increase in viewer response.

Perhaps the most moving presentation of a meditational message in recent years was seen as one segment of a series of five-minute presentations by Father Peyton's *Family Theatre*. Produced in cooperation with RKO General, the series offered thematic explorations of the Psalms, in which a number of different visualized treatments were developed as background and point of involvement during the reading of each psalm. The concept for Psalm 41, entitled "The Soldier," features actor William Shatner, who portrays a young soldier guarding a lonely stretch of beach at some unidentified battlefield. A taut and crisp series of shots follows him as he leaves his fox-hole to wade in the ocean and to share a chocolate bar with a gull. All of this is presented visually with natural sound only. As he rises from the sand to return to his fox-hole a shot rings out. He is struck. The frame freezes—and the balance of the film follows him, in extreme slow-motion and from a variety of angles, as he falls. The effect is electric, for as he begins his long fall to death a soft ethereal sound is introduced—along with a gentle and sensitive off-screen reading of the psalm. Finally, there is the poignant scene of the gull beside the fallen soldier. It is difficult to describe in words the incredible beauty and impact of this short film (which won a Venice Film Festival Award), and it ought to be commended for viewing by anyone who is charged with the task of creating short meditational and inspirational programs.

The preparation of short units which truly *televise* may be the most important service the religion program specialist can provide for the local station. The telecaster can be more flexible in assigning good air time to them, creative energy can be focused upon the development of artistic and pointed messages and the audience may be stimulated to deeper reflection. No better arguments can be made for devoting greater attention to these forms.

Children's Programs

Two distinct kinds of problems are involved in the matter of improving religious programs for children. The first group of problems relates to catching and holding the attention of young viewers and the second set of problems relates to the measure of religious truth which children can really understand. The latter involves the broader realm of educational psychology—introducing the entire matter of how children learn and grow—and requires brief analysis here.

In this connection two assumptions are in order, the first being that the religious thinking of children is not really distinct from the thinking they will apply to any other problem. Religious experience for the child is not something separate from ordinary experience. Second, it must also be noted that religious language is not factual, but poetic. Each of these assumptions must influence those who plan religious television programs for children.

Psychologists agree that certain basic elements are involved in the learning process. We experience something first through the senses, proceed to name and identify it and finally conceptualize and generalize upon it. Where religious experience is concerned, this is a secondary process, for the only way in which religious language can describe an experience is through metaphor, simile, parable and allegory. Because the child's framework of reference is more limited than the adult's, he may mistake the simile for the fact. The young child is naturally literalistic and physical in his thinking, and the language of religion has less meaning for him.

The religious program planner must therefore take into account the patterns of thinking in children from childhood through adolescence. Until the age of about four, psychologists have discovered, the child goes through a phase of prelogical thought in which he will base his judgments upon the nearest or most impressionable aspect of a problem. Then the child enters a stage of concrete logic in which he may tend to leap from one illogical aspect of a problem to another, taking them all as evidence but not connecting them logically. It is not until he develops to a third stage of thinking, namely logic which is of an abstract quality—formal operational thinking—that he can form hypotheses and begin to relate his own experience and judgment to problems which are posed.

Dr. R. J. Goldman, Senior Lecturer in Educational Psychology at England's University of Reading, has brought some of these considerations to bear upon the more specific problem of religious education:

> Approximating to prelogical thinking we had pre-religious thinking, in which the child really isn't conceiving any idea of religious

truth in the stories. In the second stage, that of concrete logic, the child is now thinking sub-religiously. The kind of theology he is able to achieve is something like the early Mosaic religion. It's concretistic, it's crude, it's physical. In the third stage, that of abstract logic, the child begins to get through to some idea of religious truth because he is at a level of what we would call personal religious thinking. He is able to hypothesis, as he would in science. He is able to think propositionally. If the question is "Why was it that Jesus refused to turn the stone into bread?"—the answer of pre-religious thinking might be "Because the Devil didn't say please. He wasn't polite enough." The answer in the second stage of sub-religious thinking might be "Because man doesn't live by bread alone." You think you have got a religious genius at the age of seven or eight, and you say "How do you mean?" "Oh," says the child "He wouldn't have any cheese or any jam to put on it, so you can't live by bread alone." Now this is very good literalism, fastening upon the concrete elements of the story in such a way that the whole story is completely distorted. The answer in the third stage personal religious thinking might be "Because He didn't want to use His power wrongly."

The conclusions drawn by Goldman as well as others who have studied the problems of religious education for young people also reflect the findings of specialists in the psychology of learning in general and need to be applied in religious programming. Before the age of seven, it is observed, the child is not capable of reviewing religious instructions at an intellectual level and must be exposed to those situations in which his experience is enriched and in which he may "feel" his way into religion. It is suggested also that the nature of religious programming should change as the child enters the second stage, from about the age of seven on, when the focus should reflect life themes and the religious content should be placed within a framework of the child's normal, natural life experience.

Obviously, the creation of programs for children in the first two stages of development present problems of a special order and developing formats in these areas requires the talents and expertise of many kinds of people, as well as the advice of educators, psychologists, religious school teachers and others who are engaged in the problem of child development. Many of the programs described in this volume put these approaches into action and may serve as models for those who contemplate religious programs for children in the lower age groups. It would also be useful to consult an earlier volume in this series, *For The Young Viewer,* in which fuller explanations of approach as well as a number of useful program examples are presented.

APPENDICES

LIST OF STATIONS

The programs described in this survey were recorded by the stations listed below.

A

Abilene, Texas, KRBC-TV
Ada, Oklahoma, KTEN
Albany, New York, WAST, W-TEN (See also Schenectady, N.Y.)
Alexandria, Minnesota, KCMT
Altoona, Pennsylvania, WFBG-TV (See also Johnstown, Pa.)
Amarillo, Texas, KFDA-TV, KGNC-TV
Anchorage, Alaska, KENI-TV
Ardmore, Oklahoma, KXII
Asheville, North Carolina, WLOS-TV (See also Greenville and Spartanburg, S.C.)
Atlanta, Georgia, WAGA-TV, WQXI-TV, WSB-TV
Austin, Texas, KHFI-TV

B

Bakersfield, California, KERO-TV
Baltimore, Maryland, WBAL-TV, WJZ-TV, WMAR-TV
Bangor, Maine, WABI-TV
Baton Rouge, Louisiana, WBRZ
Bay City, Michigan, WNEM-TV
Beaumont, Texas, KBMT (See also Port Arthur, Tex.)
Billings, Montana, KULR-TV
Binghamton, New York, WNBF-TV
Birmingham, Alabama, WBRC-TV
Bluefield, West Virginia, WHIS-TV
Boise, Idaho, KBOI-TV
Boston, Massachusetts, WBZ-TV, WHDH-TV
Bowling Green, Ohio, WBGU-TV
Bristol, Virginia, WCYB-TV (See also Johnson City, Tenn.)
Buffalo, New York, WGR-TV, WKBW-TV
Burlington, Vermont, WCAX-TV

C

Carthage-Watertown, New York, WWNY-TV
Cedar Rapids, Michigan, WMT-TV
Champaign, Illinois, WCIA
Charleston, South Carolina, WCSC-TV
Charleston, West Virginia, WSAZ-TV
Charlotte, North Carolina, WSOC-TV
Chattanooga, Tennessee, WTVC
Chicago, Illinois, WBBM-TV, WBKB-TV, WGN-TV, WMAQ-TV
Chico, California, KHSL-TV
Cincinnati, Ohio, WCET, WCPO-TV, WKRC-TV, WLW-T
Clearfield, Pennsylvania, WPSX-TV
Cleveland, Ohio, WJW-TV, WKYC-TV
Colorado Springs, Colorado, KKTV
Columbia, South Carolina, WIS-TV, WNOK-TV
Columbus, Georgia, WRBL-TV, WTVN
Columbus, Mississippi, WCBI-TV
Columbus, Ohio, WBNS-TV, WLW-C, WTVN-TV
Corpus Christi, Texas, KIII, KZTV

D

Dallas, Texas, KRLD-TV, WFAA-TV
Davenport, Iowa, WOC-TV
Dayton, Ohio, WLW-D
Daytona Beach-Orlando, Florida, WESH-TV
Decatur, Alabama, WMSI-TV
Denver, Colorado, KBTV, KLZ-TV, KRMA-TV
Des Moines, Iowa, KRNT-TV, WHO-TV
Detroit, Michigan, WJBK-TV, WWJ-TV, WXYZ-TV
Dothan, Alabama, WTVY
Durham, North Carolina, WTVD (See also Raleigh, N.C.)

E

El Dorado, Arkansas-Monroe, Louisiana, KTVE
Elkhart-South Bend, Indiana, WSJV
El Paso, Texas, KROD-TV, KTSM-TV
Evansville, Indiana, WEHT, WFIE-TV, WTVW

F

Fairbanks, Alaska, KTVF
Fargo-Grand Forks, North Dakota, KTHI-TV
Florence, South Carolina, WBTW
Fort Myers, Florida, WINK-TV
Fort Wayne, Indiana, WANE-TV, WPTA
Fort Worth, Texas, KTVT, WBAP-TV (See also Dallas, Tex.)
Fresno, California, KFRE-TV

G

Grand Island, Nebraska, KGIN-TV
Grand Junction, Colorado, KREX-TV
Grand Rapids, Michigan, WOOD-TV, WZZM-TV
Great Falls, Montana, KRTV
Green Bay, Wisconsin, WBAY-TV

Greensboro, North Carolina, WFMY-TV (See also High Point and Winston-Salem, N.C.)

Greenville, South Carolina, WFBC-TV (See also Asheville, N.C. and Spartanburg, S.C.)

Greenwood, Mississippi, WABG-TV

H

Hartford, Connecticut, WTIC-TV (See also New Britain, Conn.)

Hastings, Nebraska, KHAS-TV

Hershey, Pennsylvania, WITF-TV

High Point, North Carolina, WGHP-TV (See also Greensboro and Winston-Salem, N.C.)

Honolulu, Hawaii, KGMB-TV

Houston, Texas, KHOU-TV, KPRC-TV, KTRK-TV

Huntington, West Virginia, WSAZ-TV (See also Charleston, W. Va.)

Huntsville, Alabama, WAAY-TV

Hutchinson, Kansas, KTVH

I

Idaho Falls, Idaho, KID-TV

Indianapolis, Indiana, WFBM-TV, WISH-TV, WLW-I

J

Jackson, Mississippi, WJTV, WLBT

Jacksonville, Florida, WFGA-TV, WJXT

Jefferson City, Missouri, KRCG

Johnson City, Tennessee, WJHL-TV (See also Bristol, Va.)

Johnstown, Pennsylvania, WJAC-TV (See also Altoona, Pa.)

Jonesboro, Arkansas, KAIT-TV

K

Kalamazoo, Michigan, WKZO-TV
Kansas City, Missouri, KCMO-TV
Knoxville, Tennessee, WATE-TV, WBIR-TV

L

Lafayette, Louisiana, KLFY-TV
Lake Charles, Louisiana, KPLC-TV
Lansing, Michigan, WJIM-TV
Laredo, Texas, KGNS-TV
Las Vegas, Nevada, KORK-TV
Laurel-Hattiesburg, Mississippi, WDAM-TV
Lexington, Kentucky, WKYT-TV, WLEX-TV
Lincoln, Nebraska, KOLN-TV
Little Rock-Pine Bluff, Arkansas, KATV, KTHV
Los Angeles, California, KABC-TV, KCOP, KMEX-TV, KNBC, KTTV
Louisville, Kentucky, WAVE-TV, WHAS-TV
Lubbock, Texas, KLBK-TV
Lynchburg, Virginia, WLVA-TV

M

Mankato, Minnesota, KEYC-TV
Mason City, Iowa, KGLO-TV
Mayaguez, Puerto Rico, WORA-TV
Memphis, Tennessee, WHBQ-TV, WMC-TV, WREC-TV
Meridian, Mississippi, WTOK-TV
Miami Beach, Florida, WCKT, WLBW-TV, WTHS-TV
Midland-Odessa, Texas, KMID-TV
Milwaukee, Wisconsin, WITI-TV, WTMJ-TV
Minneapolis-St. Paul, Minnesota, KMSP-TV, KSTP-TV, WCCO-TV, WTCN-TV
Missoula, Montana, KGVO-TV
Mobile, Alabama, WALA-TV, WKRG-TV
Moline, Illinois, WQAD-TV

Monroe-West Monroe, Louisiana, KNOE-TV
Montgomery, Alabama, WKAB-TV, WSFA

N

Nashville, Tennessee, WLAC-TV, WSIX-TV, WSM-TV
New Bedford, Massachusetts, WTEV (See also Providence, R.I.)
New Bern, North Carolina, WNBE-TV
New Britain, Connecticut, WHNB-TV (See also Hartford, Conn.)
New Orleans, Louisiana, WDSU-TV, WWL-TV
New York, New York, WCBS-TV, WNBC-TV, WNDT, WOR-TV
Norfolk, Virginia, WAVY-TV, WTAR-TV

O

Oak Hill, West Virginia, WOAY-TV
Oakland-San Francisco, California, KTVU
Odessa, Texas, KOSA-TV
Oklahoma City, Oklahoma, KETA, KOCO-TV, KWTV, WKY-TV
Omaha, Nebraska, KETV, KMTV, WOW-TV
Onondaga, Michigan, WILX-TV
Orlando, Florida, WDBO-TV (See also Daytona Beach, Fla.)

P

Paducah, Kentucky, WPSD-TV
Palm Beach, Florida, WPTV
Pasco, Washington, KEPR
Peoria, Illinois, WMBD-TV
Philadelphia, Pennsylvania, WCAU-TV, WFIL-TV
Phoenix, Arizona, KOOL-TV, KPHO-TV
Pittsburgh, Pennsylvania, KDKA-TV, WIIC-TV, WTAE-TV
Ponce, Puerto Rico, WRIK-TV
Port Arthur, Texas, KJAC-TV (See also Beaumont, Tex.)
Portland, Maine, WCSH-TV
Portland, Oregon, KATU, KGW-TV, KOIN-TV
Presque Isle, Maine, WAGM-TV

Providence, Rhode Island, WJAR-TV, WPRI-TV (See also New Bedford, Mass.)

R

Raleigh, North Carolina, WRAL-TV (See also Durham, N.C.)
Richmond, Virginia, WRVA-TV, WTVR-TV
Roanoke, Virginia, WDBJ-TV, WSLS-TV
Rochester, New York, WHEC-TV, WOKR, WROC-TV
Rockford, Illinois, WREX-TV, WTVO
Rock Island, Illinois, WHBF-TV
Roswell, New Mexico, KSWS-TV

S

Sacramento, California, KXTV
St. Louis, Missouri, KMOX-TV, KSD-TV, KTVI
Salina, Kansas, KSLN
Salt Lake City, Utah, KCPX-TV, KSL-TV, KUTV
San Antonio, Texas, KENS-TV, KLRN, KSAT-TV, WOAI-TV
San Diego, California, KFMB-TV, KOGO-TV
San Francisco, California, KGO-TV, KPIX, KRON-TV, KTVU
San Jose, California, KNTV
San Juan, Puerto Rico, WKAQ-TV
Santa Barbara, California, KEYT
Santa Maria, California, KCOY-TV
Savannah, Georgia, WSAV-TV, WTOC-TV
Schenectady, New York, WREG (See also Albany, N.Y.)
Scranton, Pennsylvania, WNEP-TV (See also Wilkes-Barre, Pa.)
Seattle, Washington, KING-TV, KIRO-TV, KOMO-TV
Selma, Alabama, WSLA
Shreveport, Louisiana, KSLA-TV, KTBS-TV
Sioux City, Iowa, KVTV
Sioux Falls, South Dakota, KELO TV
South Bend-Elkhart, Indiana, WNDU-TV, WSBT-TV
Spartanburg, South Carolina, WSPA-TV (See also Asheville, N.C., Greenville, S.C.)
Spokane, Washington, KREM-TV, KXLY-TV
Springfield, Massachusetts, WHYN-TV, WWLP

Springfield, Missouri, KTTS-TV
Steubenville, Ohio-Wheeling, West Virginia, WSTV-TV

T

Tampa-St. Petersburg, Florida, WTVT
Temple-Waco, Texas, KCEN-TV
Terre Haute, Indiana, WTHI-TV
Thomasville, Georgia-Tallahassee, Florida, WCTV
Toledo, Ohio, WTOL-TV
Topeka, Kansas, WIBW-TV
Tucson, Arizona, KVOA-TV
Tulsa, Oklahoma, KOED-TV, KOTV, KVOO-TV
Tupelo, Mississippi, WTWV
Tyler, Texas, KLTV

V

Visalia, California, KICU-TV

W

Washington, District of Columbia, WRC-TV, WTOP-TV, WTTG
Wausau, Wisconsin, WSAU-TV
Weslaco, Texas, KRGV-TV
Weston, West Virginia, WDTV
Wheeling, West Virginia, WTRF-TV (See also Steubenville, Ohio)
Wichita Falls, Texas, KAUZ-TV, KFDX-TV
Wilkes-Barre, Pennsylvania, WBRE-TV (See also Scranton, Pa.)
Wilmington, North Carolina, WECT, WWAY
Winston-Salem—Greensboro, North Carolina, WSJS-TV (See also High
    Point, N.C.)

Y

Yakima, Washington, KIMA-TV
Youngstown, Ohio, WFMJ-TV, WKBN-TV, WYTV
Yuma, Arizona, KIVA

SELECTED

REFERENCES

ON RELIGIOUS

BROADCASTING

Danish, Roy. *Some Guidelines for Religious Broadcasting.* A talk given before the Catholic Communications Convention, San Francisco, California, May 9, 1966. Television Information Office, 745 Fifth Avenue, New York, N. Y. 10022. 12p. Apply.

Danish, Roy. *Some Suggestions for New Approaches to Religious Broadcasting.* Remarks at the National Methodist Communications Consultation, December 17, 1964. Television Information Office, 745 Fifth Avenue, New York, N. Y. 10022. 6p. Apply.

Dick, Donald. "Religious Broadcasting: 1920–1965. A Bibliography." *Journal of Broadcasting,* Temple University, Philadelphia, Pennsylvania 19122. Summer, 1965, pp. 249–279; Spring, 1966, pp. 163–180. Apply.

Fore, William F. *A Short History of Religious Broadcasting.* Broadcasting and Film Commission, National Council of the Churches of Christ in the U. S. A., 475 Riverside Drive, New York, N. Y. 10027. December, 1968. (mimeo) 9p. Apply.

Jackson, B. F., ed. *Communication—Learning for Churchmen.* (Communication for Churchmen, Vol. I.) Abingdon Press, 201 8th Avenue, South, Nashville, Tennessee 37202. 1968. 303p. $5.95.

Jackson, B. F., ed. *Television-Radio-Film for Churchmen.* (Communication for Churchmen, Vol. II.) Abingdon Press, 201 8th Avenue, South, Nashville, Tennessee 37202. (In preparation.) Apply.

Johnson, Philip A.; Temme, Norman; and Hushaw, Charles C., eds. *Telling the Good News: A Public Relations Handbook for Churches.* Concordia Publishing House, 3558 South Jefferson Avenue, St. Louis, Missouri 63118. 1962. 202p. $2.50.

Sellers, James E. *The Outsider and the Word of God.* Abingdon Press, 201 8th Avenue, South, Nashville, Tennessee 37202. 1961. 240p. $4.00.

A Short History of
RELIGIOUS
BROADCASTING

By WILLIAM F. FORE

Executive Director, Broadcasting and Film Commission,
National Council of Churches

Commercial radio began with the first broadcast from KDKA in East Pittsburgh, November 2, 1920, and the first religious broadcast followed soon afterward from Calvary Episcopal Church, Pittsburgh, by the Rev. Edwin Van Etten, over KDKA.

Denominational response to the fact of radio was to *buy and operate stations*. With no federal control for nearly a decade, stations battled over frequencies, and religious broadcasters battled over doctrine.

In 1923 Frank C. Goodman formed the Radio Office of the Greater New York Federation of Churches and started a schedule of three programs on New York City stations, one of them being *National Radio Pulpit* on WEAF (now WNBC), first aired May 3, 1923.

In 1923 when the NBC network was formed, *National Radio Pulpit* went "network," featuring Dr. S. Parkes Cadman in the first religious broadcast from a studio instead of remote from a church. The Federal Council of Churches was brought in as sponsor and the Council's executive, Dr. McFarland, sat on the

NBC Religious Advisory Council, which formulated the following policies: (1) religious groups should receive free time, but pay for their production costs; (2) religious broadcasting should be non-denominational; (3) use one man for continuity; (4) use a preaching format, "avoiding matters of doctrine and controversial subjects."

In 1934 the Greater New York Council relinquished responsibility for network radio to the Department of National Religious Radio of the FCCC, which then had 25 cooperating denominations and six radio programs. All formats were preaching or speaking. On Dr. Cadman's death in 1936, Dr. Ralph Sockman, who had carried the summer responsibility since 1928, became featured speaker and remained so for more than 25 years. There was little music and no drama, news for children's programming. Most participants were from the New York City area. In the early 1940's a thousand letters were being received each day in the Federal Council broadcasting office.

In 1944, the Joint Religious Radio Committee of the Congregational Christian, Methodist, Presbyterian USA Churches and the United Church of Canada were organized by the Rev. Everett C. Parker with the help of James R. Angell of NBC. This group began the first nationally-syndicated religious programs, sponsored religious-radio-workshops and cooperated with NBC in granting radio fellowships for ministers to attend summer radio institutes.

In 1945 the Protestant Film Commission was formed to coordinate efforts of film production for the 25 member denominations in the Federal Council of Churches. The first film was *Beyond Our Own,* with a budget of about $40,000. At first, denominations poured funds into film productions. A high point was reached in 1952 when 14 films were produced. From 1946 to 1952, denominational boards spent $800,000 on films. Paul Heard was the first executive and Oren Evans became Director of the Hollywood office in 1949. The PFC was the agency for almost all denominational film production and actually produced most films, putting together film crews but not owning studio facilities. In addition, the Hollywood Office reviewed, prior to production, about 75 commercial film scripts annually in the period 1949–51. The annual Green Lake Audiovisual Conference, begun in 1944, became the national center for audiovisual production and utilization training. Many denominational executives became film "producers."

In 1948 the Joint Religious Radio Committee and the Department of National Religious Radio, FCCC, merged into the Protestant Radio Commission, with Everett Parker at its head. Dramatic transcriptions were made, including the first children's show, *All Aboard For Adventure,* and the 13 quarter-hour shows, *The Radio Edition of The Bible.*

Throughout the 1930's and 1940's the Federal Council maintained a policy of requesting sustaining (i.e., unpaid for) time for itself as the major representative of Protestant Churches in America. The NBC policy was to not sell time for religious broadcasting because "such a course might result in a disproportionate representation of those individuals or groups who chance to command the largest purses." It and ABC (the old Blue Network) gave time to the three major faith groups rather than try to serve each faith group. CBS built its own religious programs, also working with the three major faith groups. The Mutual Broadcasting System had been selling time for religion. In 1944 Mutual began limiting commercial religious programs to Sunday morning, setting a maximum of a half-hour for individual shows, and forbade direct solicitation of funds over the air. The National Association of Evangelicals claimed the FCCC had driven paid religious broadcasting off the air. Actually programs such as *The Voice of Prophecy,* Dr. Charles E. Fuller's *Pilgrim Hour* and M. R. DeHaan's *Radio Bible Class* continued through audience support of the follow-up materials.

November 21, 1948 saw the origination of CBS-TV's *Lamp Unto My Feet.* What started as a Sunday school telecast is now in its third decade.

On December 6, 1950, the Broadcasting and Film Commission was organized in Cleveland, Ohio, as a special body of the newly formed National Council of Churches. Dr. Ronald Bridges, former President of the Pacific School of Religion in Berkeley,

California, was its first executive. It merged the Protestant Film Commission and the Protestant Radio Commission as equal partners.

The years 1951 and 1952 saw the pulling together of denominational broadcasting endeavors in a serious way. Format continued to rely on *personalities*—Pike, Peale, Sockman, Bonnell, Sheen.

The 1940's and early 1950's saw the development of the following FCCC radio programs: *Gems of Thought* (5 minutes daily), *Faith In Our Time* (15 minutes daily), *Religion In The News* (15 minutes Saturday), *Art of Living, Church of The Air* (CBS), *National Radio Pulpit* (NBC) and *National Vespers* (ABC). The Roman Catholics had four major programs: *The Ave Maria Hour* (drama, 120 stations on a made network) and *The Catholic Hour* (featuring Fulton Sheen on 102 stations), both NBC, *Faith In Our Times* (MBS) and *The Hour of Faith* (ABC)—all controlled by the National Council of Catholic Men. Non-NCCM programs included *Rosary Hour, Highway To Heaven* and Bishop Fulton J. Sheen's programs.

The Jewish mainstay was *The Eternal Light,* a half-hour dramatic series which employed many of the best radio writers and actors. *Eternal Light,* produced on the NBC network in cooperation with the Jewish Theological Seminary of America, continues its distinguished career today. In addition, a television version began in the 1950's on NBC-TV as part of its three-faith series.

By 1955, BFC radio included *Pulpit, The Art of Living, Good News* (a 15-minute live newscast on MBS), *Pilgrimage* (John Sutherland Bonnell, counseling), *Let There Be Light* (dramatic transcriptions), and *Thy Kingdom Come* (United Presbyterian musical series). But as radio network schedules changed (for example, NBC launching "Monitor"), station acceptance for these programs began to drop rapidly.

By the late 1940's television had become a major medium. The Protestant Radio Commission went into television in 1948 and helped found *Look Up and Live* and *Lamp Unto My Feet* (both CBS). The *Puppet Films* were released in 1951, *This Is*

The Life in 1952, and in three years denominations produced ten series for TV. *Frontiers Of Faith* (NBC) began as a church service remote, then experimented with several formats. *Look Up and Live* relied on name personalities such as Chuck Templeton and Merv Griffin. *What's Your Trouble?* starred the Peales. *Man To Man* and *The Pastor* used name preachers.

By 1954 a more sophisticated view of broadcasting was emerging. Dean Liston Pope delivered a scathing attack on religious "skits" in which "Christian family life becomes reduced to little moralisms and pleasantries," on peace-of-mind theology and on programs aimed solely at the intellectual. That same year the ABC-TV network originated a program with Bishop James Pike.

During the fifties, films continued to be made for 15 cooperating denominations, but as initial enthusiasm waned, the budgets tended to be more modest and subjects were restricted mainly to missions, stewardship and relief. In Hollywood, the BFC West Coast Office concentrated on reviewing scripts and made recommendations to producers. The BFC cooperated in the "Greensheet" review of commercial films. The Green Lake Conference became broader, dealing not just with films but with many areas of communication and education.

The fifties saw considerable placement of religious personalities on the large number of daily radio and TV interview shows. Training of ministers continued, with emphasis on techniques of using the microphone, building a local show and general "use of the media." In 1955 there were 40 one-day training institutes and 10 one-week workshops. That year also saw publication of the Parker, Barry and Smythe book, *The Television-Radio Audience and Religion,* which summarized the two-year BFC research project at Yale Divinity School, conducted at a cost of $87,500.

1956 saw an NCC Pronouncement on paid time. Its key points were: (1) church groups should provide free programs; (2) networks and stations should provide free time; (3) time should neither be bought nor sold for religious broadcasts; and (4) that marginal time given for religious broadcasts is not in the public interest and does not discharge station responsibility. The evangelical broadcasters tended to interpret this as a further attempt to get them off the air. Discussions during the next four years resulted in a "Code of Standards of 1960," consisting mainly of vague generalizations, but tending to heal somewhat the rift in BFC-evangelical broadcaster relationships.

The big budget years for religious television production were 1955–1960. In 1955 alone, production costs were:

Frontiers of Faith	$ 17,000
Look Up And Live	9,000
The Day Before Easter	36,514
Man To Man	140,000
The Pastor	55,000
The Way	225,000
This Is The Life	750,000

There followed more filmed-TV series, programs of considerable costliness, including Methodist productions of *The Way, Talk Back, The Way II, Talkback II,* plus *Off To Adventure* for children.

1957 saw publication of Malcolm Boyd's *Crisis in Communication;* 1960, John Bachman's *The Church In The World Of Radio-TV,* Martin Marty's *Improper Opinion,* James Seller's *The Outsider And The Word of God;* and 1961, Everett Parker's *Religious Television.* Among the ideas beginning to circulate by 1960:

(1) It might be better to *produce less, use existing material more* (Bachman report).

(2) "Authenticity" (Bachman, Dave Barry, Martin Marty).

(3) Broadcasting does not very often change fundamentally-held ideas (Klapper and Bachman).

(4) Need to consider the total influence of mass media on life (Cynthia Wedel).

(5) A global communications plan, pooling of all Protestant resources (Larry McMaster).

(6) Recognize the changes in the use of radio (Charles Brackbill and John Groller).

(7) Need to deal with the FCC and station's public interest responsibilities (Brackbill).

(8) Development of a master plan (S. Franklin Mack, then director of BFC).

In 1960, switching from *The Bishop Pike* series, the ABC-TV network started to work ecumenically with their *Directions* series. That year BFC members put $90,000 into *Frontiers of Faith,* with maximum control by BFC's committee. *Look Up and Live* did some of its most creative programs, such as the "Seeking Years" and "Sandpile" series. Radio audience mail continued to drop because of rising cost of handling, loss of station acceptance, and the changing role of radio. *Davey and Goliath,* the first animated series for children, produced by the Lutheran Church in America, was released for syndication through the BFC in 1961.

The 1963 NCC Pronouncement, *The Church and TV and Radio Broadcasting,* asked the industry to live up to its codes and the FCC to exercise its authority. But the lack of advance local preparation, poor press and general misunderstanding of the Pronouncement resulted in much local anguish and station repercussions. The National Religious Broadcasters group—primarily evangelical and fundamentalist organizations—continued to stress purchase of radio time.

1964–67 saw a radical rethinking of BFC functions. There was a move away from seeing the BFC as primarily a producer of films and TV shows, toward BFC as an enabler of network programs and film resources. The long-standing policy that the church should pay for broadcast production was exchanged for a policy that the networks should pay the production costs, since they were responsible for the programs in the eyes of the FCC. By 1967, BFC-TV staff was acting in a liaison relationship with each of three networks, but was still engaged directly in the production of *Pulpit, Pilgrimage* and *Art of Living,* using network facilities. This same period saw large production outlays by some denominations, principally for TV programs, while others experienced considerable cutbacks. Radio and then TV spots assumed new importance.

In 1964 BFC began to increase active engagement in government and industry relationships. A Government and Industry

Committee was created and staff spent considerable time working with the National Association of Broadcasters, the FCC and network personnel. In 1964 the BFC urged the FCC to adopt new license application forms which would stress the applicant's plans to broadcast in the public interest; the new forms which resulted allowed a much better comparison of "performance against promise." In June 1967, testimony before the House Interstate and Foreign Commerce Committee urged passage of the Public Broadcasting Bill, which did in fact become law at the end of that year. In 1968 the BFC filed comments to the FCC in support of equal employment opportunities in broadcasting, and in 1969 it filed an *amicus* brief in support of the constitutionality of the Fairness Doctrine in the CBS-Red Lion case before the Supreme Court.

During the same period there was a reversal of policies being pursued in the West Coast Office. Approval of scripts prior to production was cancelled. Educational programs were emphasized, including Pastoral Previews and film reviews. A half-time Director of Utilization function was added in 1965; this included developing the use of existing television and films by the church, communication education, a Film Awards program and the development of film reviews and training programs. Also, beginning about 1965, denominations began to experience a drop in the income available for national activities. This drop was felt throughout the NCC, including the BFC. At the end of 1966 the West Coast Office was closed and in 1967 utilization of media was cut back.

A summer conference for Council broadcast executives was inaugurated in 1963, first under the auspices of two denominations and then by the BFC. In 1965 the National Association of Council Broadcast Executives, a professional organization, was formed out of the Council Broadcasters' Fellowship which had functioned since the early 1950's. The Catholic Broadcasters Association, an affiliation of diocesan broadcasters, had begun in 1948.

In 1966 a Director of Field Service was loaned part-time by the United Presbyterian Church to the BFC as an experiment, but this was discontinued because of costs. The Presbyterian Field Staff also was cut back about the same time, although interest in building a strong relationship between denominations and council broadcasters remained high. The BFC began to sponsor two meetings a year of Council broadcast executives and denominational leaders; by 1968 the meeting had Catholic, Jewish and Canadian representation as well. Beginning in 1967, a considerable number of laymen in the fields of broadcasting and film were added to the BFC for the first time, both on the Board of Managers and in the operating committees.

As the emphasis on "church production" diminished, a new emphasis took its place: news and special events. The BFC established a Broadcast News operation in mid-1968, the purpose of which was to interpret the life and witness of the church to the broadcast media. Ever since Vatican II, the church *was* news. News had been assuming a new importance in network and local radio and TV as well. The new BFC staff developed an information-gathering process for input to the networks and fed important stories via wire to local council of churches broadcast executives for local placement. At the same time, BFC network programs tended to deal more and more with the moral implications of the significant social issues of the day.

In 1965 the National Catholic Office for Radio and Television was created by the bishops of the United States. In 1968 NCORT became a part of the new Communication Department of the United States Catholic Conference and at the same time was declared to be responsible for *all* Catholic broadcast responsibilities, thus ending the long history of network relationships which the National Conference of Catholic Men had maintained.

Serious joint Protestant-Catholic planning of television programming began in 1965. The first joint film award with the National Catholic Office of Motion Pictures was made in 1967, and the first joint financing of network religious programs in 1968. 1968 also saw the first local Protestant-Catholic financing of religious programming in Connecticut, San Francisco and Detroit. In early 1969 the Connecticut Council of Churches announced a fully ecumenical broadcast operation, as many state and local councils of churches changed their names and structures to allow full participation by the Roman Catholic Church.

INDEX

BV656.3
.B55

Bluem, William

PERS
2~4.3
BLU

PS
3

RELIGIOUS TELEVISION PROGRAMS

Bluem, William
Religious Television
Programs

BV656.3
.B55

22991